RESTAURANT STRONG

The 5 first principles of
restaurant category leadership

SECOND EDITION

RESTAURANT STRONG

The 5 first principles of restaurant category leadership

PETER LESAR

DineRock™

Published by DineRock™
DineRock™ is a registered trademark.
Printed in the United States of America.
ISBN: 978-1-969338-59-5

For more information, please write:
DineRock
3118 W Barcelona St. Tampa, FL 33629
Visit us online at: www.dinerock.com

Read Here First:

Restaurant “category leaders” are those who dominate in market share in their category, and they often earn as much as their next 7-9 direct competiitors...combined.

Restaurant Strong unveils the 5 *timeless* first principles every single category leader has relied on to emerge from once humble start-up to global brand.

DineRock, the company behind *Restaurant Strong*, is an accelerator that mentors and invests in restaurant businesses. We already accelerate many great brands. Learn more about us at www.DineRock.com. If you have inquiries, you may contact the author Peter LeSar at peter@agility.capital (Agility Capital is the publicly traded owner of DineRock).

CONTENTS

INTRODUCTION

BRIDGING YOUR PERFORMANCE GAP

Category leader = Restaurant company that generates the most revenue and income within its cuisine type & service format.

THERE IS A PERFORMANCE GAP between you and the world's independent and chain restaurant category leaders.

That gap can only be bridged by knowledge about restaurant outperformance that they have earned and that you seek.

Over the years, you[1] and your team have become *tactical* experts on how to develop and run a restaurant.[2] That know-how has helped your company to serve the needs of customers, but it hasn't been enough to bridge your business realities to your highest aspirations. That is because while there are countless tactics one could learn in our business, each on its own is relatively easy to master.

Insight #1: Tactics have a low value compared to other forms of knowledge and offer no map to sustained outperformance.

1 I address *you* as an individual or as a team reading this book together.

2 I use the word "restaurant" to refer to a single restaurant, a group or a chain—interpret the word for your situation.

Over the years, you have also gained *strategic* knowledge through observation of category leaders. Time permitting, you follow their moves in search of kernels of truth to help bridge your way to your business and life goals. You are not alone in this practice. Executives, chefs, owners, investors and marketers in every segment and corner of our planet do the same. Unfortunately, it has been hard for you to adopt the strategies of category leaders to transform your business outcomes. That is because strategies are just a sequence of tactics that can be copied by anyone who focuses on them.

Insight #2: A strategy also rarely offers an enduring competitive advantage.

The observation and adoption of tactics and strategies deployed by others will always be hit or miss unless founded in *timeless first principles* of how greatness and great financial outcomes unfold. First principles transcend changes in technology, culture and markets as *the* building blocks of understanding that underpin all other knowledge. The greatest philosophical arguments of Aristotle, Confucius, Descartes and the greatest discoveries of Einstein, Newton and Darwin can all be described as first principles.

First principles are the baseline of *what matters most* from which *what works best* emerges—including in restaurants. When you observe category leaders such as Chick-fil-A, Starbucks, Noma and The French Laundry and try to divine how they have succeeded to such heights, you *informally* search for first principles of restaurant outperformance. And yet, even though millions of us seek outperformance knowledge above all else in our business, there has never been a formal study of category leaders as a group to see if there are indeed universal principles of how and why they outperform.

Restaurant Strong answers this question.

As they navigated from ordinary to extraordinary, what timeless first principles of outperformance have category leaders uncovered that can help you to rise across that space as well?

You are about to read the first study ever done on how category leaders across time, geography and segment have risen to greatness and great financial outcomes. In the history of dining, only a handful of independent restaurants and founders have emerged as international icons, and only a smattering of chains have risen to become global power houses. Because nobody before had ever isolated our industry's category leaders for study, a knowledge gap around how outperformance can be purposefully designed into restaurants has almost certainly short changed the outcomes of your company.

Here is the enduring truth of this book:

Insight #3: The same exact *principles* connect the rise up and enduring outperformance of every category leader from our most globally renowned independent restaurants to the world's largest restaurant chains.

I have obsessively studied category leaders for over a decade, comparing and contrasting their behaviors to those of the rest. I have carved back the unessential, the less-than-universal and the ephemeral, trendy approaches that lead restaurants down false paths. Here is what I have learned:

1. Widely held mistruths promote sub-optimal outcomes for approximately 97% of restaurant brands.[3]

---

[3] Calculated by dividing the number of nationally and internationally recognized independent and chain brands in multiple markets and market types by the number of all identifiable restaurant brands in each market. In all cases, the number of leading brands was between 1% and 4% of the total market, while the average was 3%.

2. A handful of first principles guide approximately 3% of brands, restaurant category leaders, up the ramp to greatness and great financial results.
3. And, whether you wish to lift a restaurant that has matured or revive one out of crisis, *the first principles to great outcomes are the same in all cases*.

After years of separating out mistruth from first principles, I tested the latter in my first restaurant[4] with an investment of just $140,000. The result: It was named by The World's 50 Best Restaurants™ Discovery Series as one of 50 "*next generation dining destinations*"[i] around the globe. It was described in Bloomberg as "*the most memorable meal of the year*"[ii] and in Lonely Planet as the "*hottest reservation*" of its market. My next restaurant, with an investment of less than $50,000, was named as one of the "*15 best new restaurant openings*"[iii] throughout the Americas. Though we had neither a media nor marketing budget, press from around the world wrote about us and guests paid up front, often months in advance, to dine with us.

I developed these two humble restaurants with a line cook named José (now a world class chef) and my long-time friend Alberto.[iv] We did so with neither an interior designer nor industry consultant of any kind, and we opened in what was gang territory at the time in a market far removed from all culinary maps. Despite small investments and outsized disadvantages, the excitement we generated confirmed to me that a monumental idea for our industry was afoot:

> *First principles show a path to extraordinary results in our business, and that path can be progressed along by any of us.*

This book documents the **The 5 First Principles of Restaurant Category Leadership.** My research has looked at over 100 of the

[4] First restaurant of mine outside of our publicly traded company.

world's most renowned restaurant brands and restaurateurs across all segments. In doing so, I learned that even among category leaders, only the very top performers pursue all of the principles in this book. The rest only work with some of these principles and it is reflected in their outcomes. How much you commit will determine your outcomes as well.

My goal is that the knowledge herein sharply raises the very expectations of what you believe is possible for you and your business. Exciting growth can re-start at any time. I have seen it under all conditions imaginable and firmly believe that *multiple levels up* of financial performance and impact are well within your restaurant company's reach.

CHAPTER 1

DIMINISHING INTEREST PRINCIPLE

The biggest restaurant challenge...and how to solve it.

MY FRIEND SRINIDHI FROM THE restaurant business in India will often say with a grin of irony that this or that local place "is *world* famous *only* in Mumbai." His twist of language shines light on a quirk of the restaurateur's nature: We see our restaurant(s) at the center of the narrative and often fail to perceive what is different without exception about those few restaurant brands that continually outperform our own. In other words, we are blinded by *biases* that limit our ability to make serious progress with our businesses.

When did today's restaurant category leaders start to emerge as leaders? When they learned to better filter for truth. You have biases that you don't see, and now is when we begin to knock them down in domino fashion.

WHERE WE ALL GET STUCK

"Guys, what the heck is wrong?" I asked our restaurant management team. "We aren't growing proportional to the efforts we all put in. Any thoughts?"

Solemn faces.

I was an American expat running the Asian operations of a publicly traded hospitality company. We had opened up 5 restaurants in the region by then. My team was international, experienced and there were managers, chefs and marketers at the table. Our results were soft even though we collectively *believed* we had done many things right. We had solid locations, offered value for money, served crave-able food and provided consistent service from a portfolio of targeted brands. And yet none of them were great businesses.

A knowledge gap we had is in not recognizing that there is one dominating Growth Model that category leaders integrate into their practices to emerge as leaders in the first place. This book, via first principles, will unfold this growth model for you in exactly the order you must think about it vis-a-vis your own business. At the core of this Restaurant Growth Model is the insight that you must buy into above all others:

> **Insight #4: Growth rate is the foundational solution to every restaurant challenge and opportunity before you. Ensuring that your business is structured to promote a higher rate of growth than your competitors for even decades must be your highest priority.**

Why is that? Because your *revenue growth rate and how high it remains* for years on end relative to competitors is what lifts *relative* capital accumulation, and relative capital accumulation solves all other challenges. Restaurant revenue in your market is finite and you are in a quiet battle for customers with other restaurants and emerging types of competition. If you have a slower growth rate than those of competitors, they will ever-accrue more resources to raise the competitive bar and you will eventually have trouble keeping up. The same applies in reverse. You need to outpace competitors continuously over the long term in order to accumulate the capital you need to realize the biggest goals you have for yourself and your business.

If you don't achieve this outcome you will always face challenges you can't resolve simply because you will be comparatively under resourced rather than relatively over resourced. The point: All of your worries are subsets of your revenue growth rate challenge. If you leave that challenge behind, your other challenges also fall to the wayside. Does that make sense? Therefore, the purpose of this chapter is to *bridge your knowledge gap* between:

GUESSING HOW TO GROW ··········► KNOWING HOW TO GROW

The restaurants in our company had many moving parts that made them difficult to manage and scale. We worked hard to make the *in*efficient...well, efficient. We simplified operations, training and procurement. We flattened our chain of command and empowered people on the ground to make decisions. For a while we made real progress, but eventually each new effort produced *diminishing returns* in efficiency. It was like squeezing an orange...the first few squeezes produce a lot of juice but, at some point, you squeeze harder than before and get far less out of it. The challenge: How could we grow income if our revenues were flat and we had no more juice to squeeze out of our expenses?

Eventually, I remembered something I had said many times. *If you tackle an obstacle harder than anyone, eventually you will transform it into a competitive advantage because most people never stay the course*. I understood that diminishing returns hurt restaurants in numerous ways (as you will see), and had always assumed there was nothing anyone could do about it. Wanting to be true to my words, I decided to research how the world's category leaders tackle diminishing returns.

It was the right move.

Prepare for a winding journey of insight that at chapter's end rewards you with a graph called the *Restaurant Growth Model™*. This graph is likely the most important one you will ever see and use in your business. It lays out the big picture of how to build and sustain higher rates of revenue growth—just like the world's independent and chain category leaders have.

We will start small.

INITIAL EXCITEMENT VS. ENDURING INTEREST

Have you ever taken a first bite of something and thought "Wow, that's incredible," but after a few bites no longer notice the flavor as much? This happens to your restaurant customers and to you as well. We all have a *diminishing* appreciation of flavor the more we consume something.

Thomas Keller, founder of The French Laundry, captures this idea of diminishing enjoyment in a great interview with the renowned Powell's Books:

> *"On a hot day, that first cold beer tasted really good. By the time you got to the second or third one, they weren't so good anymore. Where do I want you to be after you've eaten something [at The French Laundry]? I want you to be thinking, 'God I wish I had a little more of that.'"*

Keller concludes by saying *"The law of diminishing returns is the most important part of that."* Under his perspective, this law looks like the graph below:[5]

[5] This and all graphs in this book are provided in printable format when you text JOIN to +1-813-669-4342. Feel free to use them as management tools and to align your team to your thinking.

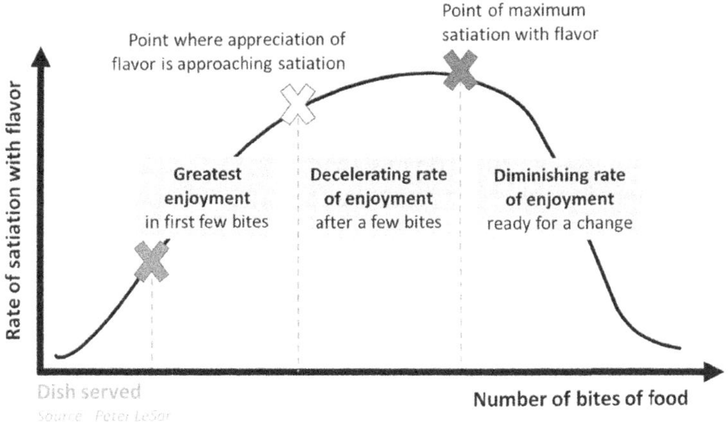

The graph shows that taste is optimal for only your first few bites. After that, you no longer enjoy the flavor as much and may eventually barely notice it. You likely experience this phenomenon with every meal you eat. It is a universal human experience, but one for which The French Laundry has a two-step workaround:

- *The first step is to capture your attention*: When serving each dish, The French Laundry wants to immediately excite your senses. Keller and his team want the presentation by staff, the plating, the ingredients and the aroma to focus your attention on the dish, and for you to be drawn into it.
- *The second step is to sustain your interest*: The French Laundry knows that no matter how incredible and novel a dish, your interest in it will diminish with each bite. To sustain your interest in the meal as a whole, the team plates only a few bites of food in each dish. Rather than "trying to pack the plate" with food and risk you losing interest, Keller gives you just enough in each dish to leave you feeling "God, I wish I had a little more of that."

In other words:

Before enjoyment of an *individual dish* diminishes, Keller cuts it off with small portions and then introduces a new novel dish so that he can push back the point in which the customer's enjoyment of the *overall meal* diminishes.

Underlying this concept is the following broader insight:

> **Insight #5: A human's interest must first be captured and second sustained, which are two very different processes. If your restaurant isn't outstanding at capturing *excitement* and then sustaining customer *interest*, you cannot outpace the revenue growth rates of others for long.**

How you excite the market into seeing your brand as a standout above all of the noise of the market *and then* how you keep the market excited long term are approaches that you will come to understand as you read coming chapters. First, you must learn the Diminishing Principle.

LAW OF DIMINISHING MARGINAL RETURNS

Diminishing returns were first discussed in economic circles in the 1700s, including by Adam Smith who is known as the *father of capitalism*. The law of diminishing marginal returns, according to Investopedia, states that: "Adding an additional factor of production results in smaller increases in output."

In Keller's example, he noted that each additional bite of a dish (factor of production) results in smaller amounts of enjoyment (output). Running with Keller's perspective, here is how we apply this law simply in this chapter:

The more you have of something, the less you value it.

Put that way, you will see moments in your life when this has happened. As an example, you were excited the first few times you drove a car, but the more you drove the less you were excited as compared to those early times. Diminishing enjoyment also happens the more you listen to a song and the more days in a row you eat pizza. Right?

As you will see below, diminishing interest or enjoyment applies in many ways in restaurants. After we review those ways and the impact of them on your business, we will come back to Keller for a surprise ending to the chapter.

DIMINISHING INTEREST BREAKS HABITS

Humans are creatures of habit, aren't we? It is a common belief we have and it seems evident when we observe our own lives. We love to eat at the same restaurants and we often order the same meal as just one example. In general, there are things we like and, while we are capable of change, we tend to lock ourselves into routines and patterns. Sort of.

Whenever I visited Hong Kong in my Asia days, I would walk to a dim sum restaurant a mile from my hotel. Along the way, I would see children heading to school, young professionals rushing for public transport and shopkeepers going through their pre-opening rituals. Then, at the restaurant, the click and clack of steamed and pan-fried dim sum always excited my hunger. Together, the walk and restaurant were immersive experiences and became habit for me.

Until eventually I just stopped going.

The walk and restaurant were still enjoyable, but I had sufficiently experienced them...it was time to try something new. My habit was broken by diminishing returns because the benefit I derived from the restaurant and walk decreased the more often that I experienced them.

> **Insight #6: *Most customers' interest* in a restaurant diminishes the more that they**

experience it. Habit organically undoes itself overtime, which has suppressed your revenue growth rate far more than you realize.

This insight might make you think about customers who have been loyal for years, and have *not* diminished their interest in your restaurant. You are right, there is always a customer base that remains more loyal and whose business is valuable as expressed through the oft-quoted Gartner Group data that:

"80% of your company's future revenue will come from just 20% of your existing customers."[v]

Those loyal customers are your valuable core, but what about the other 80%? They were *excited* to try you out, ate with you once or even many times and then their *interest* in your restaurant diminished and you lost out on far more income than you produce today. You lost income because you did not fully understand how to sustain customer interest. How much income have you lost? According to a Bain & Co. analysis as published in the *Harvard Business Review*:

"Companies can boost profits by almost 100% by retaining just 5% more of their customers."[vi]

Do the math because it's crazy. The above means that the estimated 80% of customers who have diminished away from you have taken with them *theoretically* up to 1,600%[6] more income than you currently have.[7] Now, no restaurant, not even

---

[6] Divide the 80% of your customers who have diminished away by 5% that you recover and retain as new loyal customers, and then take the resulting 16 and multiply it by 100% of income gain. The 1,600% result is theoretical as it implies absolute loyalty, but does show that we all have *higher income ceilings by multiples more* than we think.

[7] By diminished customers, I mean people who have dined or ordered out with you, but no longer do. Diminished customers include those who were once loyal and no longer are. This happens more often than you realize.

Starbucks or Chick-fil-A,[8] can sustain absolute loyalty from all of their customers, but the point is still very real:

> **Insight #7: If you could *reverse* diminishing interest, your income could grow to *at least* several multiples higher than its current level.**

You need to internalize that your diminished customers hold greater income potential than your *existing* loyal ones just by sheer numbers. I am not speaking *yet* about new customers, but just to the impact of flipping your diminishing customers to loyal ones. Please now review this:

> **Insight #8: Consumers in high-to-low order of income potential are: a) New customers (NCs) who are your growth pool; b) Diminished customers (DCs) who you need to convert to loyal ones; and c) Your *existing* loyal customers (LCs) who you need to keep happy so that they don't diminish.**

Your restaurant is likely only skillful at retaining existing LCs, but not at attracting large numbers of NCs, re-attracting large numbers of DCs and converting of both at high rates to new LCs. Retention of your existing LCs is a great skill, but not enough to produce the financial outcomes to which you aspire as there will always be leakage from once loyal customers whose habits change. This book will show you how to optimize arrivals of NCs and DCs, and how to convert as many of them as possible to lifelong LCs. *Your key to high revenue growth rates is the volume of NCs and DCs you attract and the percentage rate at which you convert them to loyal ones.* For now, let's discuss a couple more points before we draw this chapter together.

---

[8] The ability of these two chains to two-step increase their customer acquisition rate *and* reduce the diminishing rate of existing customers is what has driven their success.

RESTAURANT GROWTH CURVES

Our company was publicly traded and rigorously audited so we produced tons of data. Like you, our job was to sort for the data that mattered most and to look for trends by tracking it over time. Simple right?

It is if you are looking at "lagging indicators", meaning the *historical trends* of your business that include such bread & butter data as: How are sales this year as compared to last year? How are our prime costs as compared to industry benchmarks? How did we perform last month against budget? And so on.

The problem is that lagging indicators do *not* tell you how to mitigate risks of future revenue loss or how to build new revenue. Shaping revenue requires "leading indicators" that help us to anticipate *coming trends* that you can adjust for in advance to take advantage of them. As a simplistic example, if you knew six months before a pandemic was coming or knew for some other reason that demand in your market would weaken, you could take steps in advance to strengthen revenues in those areas of your business that perform best in those scenarios.

Macro trends are shaped by external forces (such as economic cycles or wars or pandemics) that you can't reliably predict. A trend you can easily predict, however, is one that is *the most impactful* in our business and is experienced by every restaurant in the world bar none. This predictable trend is the one that *most determines whether you achieve ordinary or extraordinary outcomes*, and is easy to spot with a leading indicator that is drawn from the only data set you likely watch every day—your revenue. Let me explain.

While researching category leaders I was also looking for leading indicators that might show me a better way to leverage our company's data. One request I made of our finance group was to show us our *rate of revenue growth* since we started. By "rate", I mean percentage growth and not actual revenues. Each restaurant's historical growth rate graph looked like this:

REVENUE GROWTH RATE CURVE

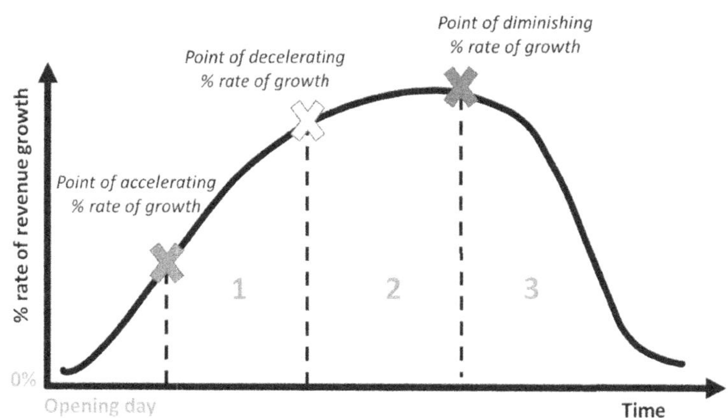

Source: Peter LeSar

For each of our restaurants, our revenue growth rate started off strong (because revenue before opening day was zero so any growth from there resulted in a high percentage increase), but eventually *decelerated* and then *diminished* until we more or less had a growth rate similar to the market rate at that time.

Think about a restaurant you have opened. It had a high revenue growth rate in the first 1-5 years, then the growth rate slowed and eventually fell to a level that was similar to that of your competitors—which rate was largely determined by how fast or slow your market was growing. That pattern you experienced was the same pattern we experienced in every restaurant of ours and that *almost* every restaurant in the world has experienced.

This pattern mimics the behavior seen in the law of diminishing marginal returns. Yes, that's right. When your revenue tapered from its initial high rate of growth, you were watching diminishing marginal returns in action being driven by two underlying trends that negatively impact every restaurant.

The first underlying trend, as already discussed, is that most of your customers (i.e., 80% of them) diminished their interest in your restaurant over time, which eventually pushed down your growth rate. The second underlying trend is that:

> **Insight #9: *Market interest* in your restaurant also diminishes (less media, less buzz, perceived less novelty) the longer you are open, meaning that your ability to acquire new customers diminishes over time as well.**

Here is the cruel reality of these two underlying trends when brought together (by understanding the trends, we can fix them):

> **Insight #10: Revenue growth rates trend down toward market averages over time because your falling ability to acquire new customers and convert them to loyal ones eventually can no longer materially outpace the revenue lost from diminishing ones.**

With this understanding, here is how to read each section of the graph above:

- *Section one*: When a restaurant first opens for business with no revenue, new customers pour in and they drive a high growth rate as you go from zero loyal customers to a growing number of them.
- *Section two*: Over time, new customer acquisition slows as novelty wears off. This results in fewer new loyal customers, but in this phase your new loyal customer production is still materially higher than your rate of diminishing ones—thus your growth rate only slows down.
- *Section three*: The further away a restaurant is from its opening date, the more its novelty wears down until it is simply no longer novel. At that point, your new customer acquisition rate falls further until eventually the number of loyal customers you are able to convert approaches

your rate of diminishing customers and the inevitable happens: Your revenue growth rate automatically drops toward a market rate of growth.

This net balance between new customer acquisition and the diminishing rate of existing customers *always* plays out this way as shown in the Revenue Growth *Rate* Curve. It is inevitable. The result is the *one Everest-sized challenge* that every restaurant on the planet shares, which is that each has an inevitable cap on revenue that looks like this:

REVENUE GROWTH CURVE IN CURRENCY TERMS

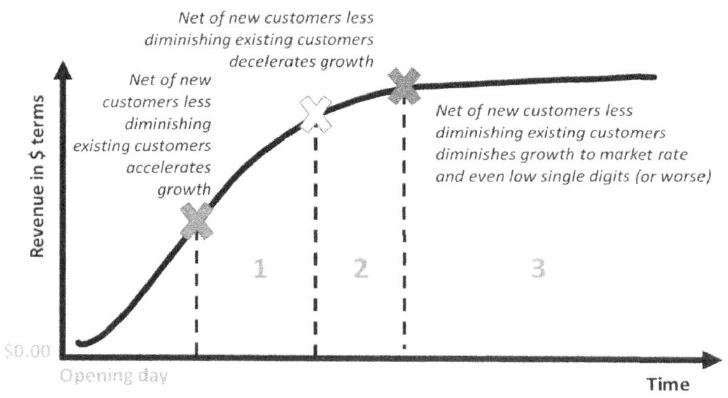

Source: Peter LeSar

As a restaurant's growth rate flattens, its rate of inflation-adjusted revenue growth in *currency* terms moves closer and closer to zero. This might take years and is subject to economic cycles, but the outcome is almost always the same unless you leverage the one long-term proven Restaurant Growth Model summarized below and laid out for you in this book. It is this model of growth that is used by every category leader of every format, from fast food to fine dining, and in every country I have ever observed. Moreover, there is no other growth model that consistently outperforms the market year-after-year for even decades on end. Period.

To clarify the math underlying the Restaurant Growth Model, please see this equation hinted at previously that describes how the growth of every restaurant rises, tapers or falls:

RG (revenue growth) = NCs (new customer spending) + LCs (loyal customer spending) – DC (lost consumption from diminishing customers)

Or, more succinctly: RG = NCs + LCs – DCs.[9] As long as new and diminished customers convert to more spending from LC conversions than spending is lost from diminishing customers, you are fine. Restaurants fail, however, when you convert insufficient numbers of loyal ones to replace lost revenue from diminishing ones for so long that "managing your cash" teeters into business closure.

Managing the balance between NCs, LCs and DCs determines when restaurants skyrocket, stagnate, falter or fail because it underlies the pace and direction of your revenue growth rate—positive or negative.

Here is a first hint at how to permanently fix the NC+LC-DC net balance in favor of higher rates of revenue growth:

> **Insight #11: The Revenue Growth Rate Curve is *the leading indicator* of when the NC+LC-DC net balance will stagnate and lose health, and alerts you in advance that it is time to intervene to re-establish a healthy balance.**

Why are category leaders able to sustain faster growth than everyone else? Why are you not able to do the same? Because they know *when* and *how* to intervene to keep the NC+LC-DC balance healthy for even decades, and you do not. The *when*

9 You should post this formula somewhere so that you and your team see it every day. You should lead management meetings by discussing how you are business building around this formula. It is *the* math formula that most determines a restaurant's outcomes.

involves intervening every time your growth rate decelerates so that it never diminishes to the level of the market. You will soon learn how this works, but what I will show you first is how the Restaurant Growth Model breaks the cruel gravity of both Restaurant Growth Curves.

Let's look at the math of it all.

MATH PATH OF CATEGORY LEADERS

The math that you sweat about every day in your restaurant is fixable: food costs can be lowered, labor reduced, utilities made more efficient and so on. These are important items that do have a positive or negative impact on your earnings, but their ranges are limited and your tinkering with them will not dramatically alter your business and life trajectory. Why is that?

There are two reasons actually.

First, the market is more powerful than expense cuts:

Let's say you roll up your sleeves and manage to reduce expenses by 3% of your revenue. If you have a million-dollar restaurant, that is $30 thousand a year saved or $2,500 a month. A solid result in a vacuum.

But markets are fluid and there are no vacuums. While you are cutting expenses, somebody else is dropping prices. Another is investing in décor and just hired a better chef. Two others upped their ad spend. Within months of you reducing expenses, the market forces you to reallocate those newly freed up resources to other areas just to keep up with competitors. And when you look back twelve months later you will see that your overall gains in income from those cuts are not $2500 a month at all, but something less.

Again, this happens because markets are fluid, but also because the restaurant business is highly competitive. Everyone strives continuously to get ahead and, in doing so, reduces the impact of the positive moves you make in your own restaurant (as do your moves reduce the impact of theirs). If disposable income for dining out was unlimited, it wouldn't matter. But the collective market size for restaurant consumption is finite. It might grow a bit in one year, or fall in the next, but growth is usually limited to low-to-mid single percentage points except in infrequent years of unbalanced inflationary boom or bust. The result: You are in a constant market share battle in which competition requires that you re-allocate expense cut savings to other items to stay competitive. That is the first reason why tinkering with expenses, while helpful, will not dramatically change your outcomes. But the reality is more brutal than that.

Second, even if you pocket that reduced expense for twenty years, it's not enough:

"Hold on a second. $30 thousand a year for twenty years is $600 thousand. How can you say that it is not enough?" I am *not* going to make the standard arguments about taxes or about real dollars when adjusting for inflation. Rather, I am going to show that in a market in which a small percentage of restaurants outperform all others in the math that matters most, you won't be able to keep up. It's time to show you the money in our business. Your *only* math path to greatness is as said:

> **Insight #12: Your revenue growth rate year-after-year must always outperform those of your direct competitors. Hitting this metric for years on end is how we define the term *"great financial outcomes"* in this book because it has a knock-on effect for all other financial outcomes you care about.**

Please note that I am not saying your revenue growth rate must always be above some artificial number as this is dependent on too many things outside of your control. I am saying that your revenue growth rate must always outperform *your direct competitors* as this is in your control as you will soon see (hard to believe that statement, but the category leader case studies in this book will make you a believer).

Let's start with your income:

Imagine two identical restaurants, each with a million dollars in revenue and the same cost structure in their base year. They are basically the same restaurant, with the only difference that our Base Case Model has a revenue growth rate of 4% on average over 20 years and the Higher Growth Model has a revenue growth rate that is just 3 points higher per year, or 7% on average.

You will remember that under our 3% expense cutting scenario, the *maximum* additional pre-tax income you will generate over twenty years is $600 thousand. Under the 3% revenue growth rate variance scenario, however, the *minimum* additional pre-tax income you would generate is $2.75 million over those same twenty years to reinvest, hire better staff, and to distribute to shareholders. See the tables below as reference. Highlighted on the far left of each table are their annual growth rates, with a 3% spread between them. The cells highlighted in the column to the left of year one show the percentage of sales applied to that line item. The two restaurants are identical in cost structure except that five expense items from the Higher Growth Restaurant are forecasted to grow at 6% rather than 7% to *conservatively* reflect the economies of scale of higher growth.

THE ONLY MATH PATH TO GREATNESS: REVENUE GROWTH RATE[10]

	BASE CASE RESTAURANT						
	Years		1	5	10	15	20
	Food	70%	$ 700,000	$ 818,901	$ 996,318	$1,212,174	$1,474,794
Growth Rate	Beverage	30%	$ 300,000	$ 350,958	$ 426,994	$ 519,503	$ 632,055
4%	**Total Revenue**		**$1,000,000**	**$1,169,859**	**$1,423,312**	**$1,731,676**	**$2,106,849**
	Food Costs	32%	$ 224,000	$ 262,048	$ 318,822	$ 387,896	$ 471,934
	Beverage Costs	25%	$ 75,000	$ 87,739	$ 106,748	$ 129,876	$ 158,014
	Totals CoGs		**$ 299,000**	**$ 349,788**	**$ 425,570**	**$ 517,771**	**$ 629,948**
	Gross Profit		**$ 701,000**	**$ 820,071**	**$ 997,742**	**$1,213,905**	**$1,476,901**
	Gross Margin %		*70%*	*70%*	*70%*	*70%*	*70%*
	Salaries & Wages	25%	$ 250,000	$ 292,465	$ 355,828	$ 432,919	$ 526,712
	Employee Benefits	5%	$ 50,000	$ 58,493	$ 71,166	$ 86,584	$ 105,342
	Direct Operating Expense	5%	$ 50,000	$ 58,493	$ 71,166	$ 86,584	$ 105,342
	Administrative Costs & Fees	3%	$ 30,000	$ 35,096	$ 42,699	$ 51,950	$ 63,205
	Marketing Expense	6%	$ 60,000	$ 70,192	$ 85,399	$ 103,901	$ 126,411
	Energy & Utilities	4%	$ 40,000	$ 46,794	$ 56,932	$ 69,267	$ 84,274
	General & Administrative	8%	$ 80,000	$ 93,589	$ 113,865	$ 138,534	$ 168,548
	Occupancy Costs	6%	$ 60,000	$ 70,192	$ 85,399	$ 103,901	$ 126,411
	Repairs & Maintenance	2%	$ 20,000	$ 23,397	$ 28,466	$ 34,634	$ 42,137
	EBITDA $		**$ 61,000**	**$ 71,361**	**$ 86,822**	**$ 105,632**	**$ 128,518**

Source: Peter LeSar

	HIGHER GROWTH RESTAURANT						
	Years		1	5	10	15	20
	Food	70%	$ 700,000	$ 917,557	$1,286,921	$1,804,974	$2,531,569
Growth Rate	Beverage	30%	$ 300,000	$ 393,239	$ 551,538	$ 773,560	$1,084,958
7%	**Total Revenue**		**$1,000,000**	**$1,310,796**	**$1,838,459**	**$2,578,534**	**$3,616,528**
	Food Costs	32%	$ 224,000	$ 293,618	$ 411,815	$ 577,592	$ 810,102
	Beverage Costs	25%	$ 75,000	$ 98,310	$ 137,884	$ 193,390	$ 271,240
	Totals CoGs		**$ 299,000**	**$ 391,928**	**$ 549,699**	**$ 770,982**	**$1,081,342**
	Gross Profit		**$ 701,000**	**$ 918,868**	**$1,288,760**	**$1,807,552**	**$2,535,186**
	Gross Margin %		*70%*	*70%*	*70%*	*70%*	*70%*
6%	Salaries & Wages	25%	$ 250,000	$ 315,619	$ 422,370	$ 565,226	$ 756,400
6%	Employee Benefits	5%	$ 50,000	$ 63,124	$ 84,474	$ 113,045	$ 151,280
6%	Direct Operating Expense	5%	$ 50,000	$ 63,124	$ 84,474	$ 113,045	$ 151,280
	Administrative Costs & Fees	3%	$ 30,000	$ 39,324	$ 55,154	$ 77,356	$ 108,496
	Marketing Expense	6%	$ 60,000	$ 78,648	$ 110,308	$ 154,712	$ 216,992
	Energy & Utilities	4%	$ 40,000	$ 52,432	$ 73,538	$ 103,141	$ 144,661
6%	General & Administrative	8%	$ 80,000	$ 100,998	$ 135,158	$ 180,872	$ 242,048
6%	Occupancy Costs	6%	$ 60,000	$ 75,749	$ 101,369	$ 135,654	$ 181,536
	Repairs & Maintenance	2%	$ 20,000	$ 26,216	$ 36,769	$ 51,571	$ 72,331
	EBITDA $		**$ 61,000**	**$ 103,635**	**$ 185,146**	**$ 312,929**	**$ 510,163**
	Annual EBITDA Variance		$ -	$ 32,274	$ 98,324	$ 207,297	$ 381,645
	Cumulative EBITDA Variance			$ 76,086	$ 421,901	$1,219,427	**$2,747,114**

Source: Peter LeSar

10 These tables, in a format you can sensitize for your own same store growth rate, are available for you for free as previously mentioned.

In the bottom right corner of the tables above is the cumulative EBITDA variance of $2.75 million.[11] The point is that a *continuously higher revenue growth rate is the only real math path to great financial outcomes.* Now you might be thinking: "You are misleading in your comparison. Under the earlier scenario of a 3% reduction in expenses, you could assume the restaurant cut its expenses in more than one year." Let's be real. I have cut expenses in many businesses, but it only happens year-after-year when falling demand enables you to keep reducing expenses that are no longer required. Continuing material levels of expense reduction aren't possible in a stable or growing restaurant because there are limits to what you can cut while still remaining competitive. Revenue growth rate is so much more valuable than expense cuts precisely because:

> **Insight #13: There is a hard floor on how much expenses can be cut, but theoretically there is no ceiling on how much revenue can grow over time. Also, higher growth facilitates greater expense cuts (as a percentage of sales) through economies of scale than does cutting the expenses of a stagnate business.**[12]

Therefore, it's best for your *income* that you invest most of your time into revenue growth over all else (this book shows you how to invest that growth time wisely). You might think your market size or operating capacity imposes revenue limits, and you would be

---

11 EBITDA equals earnings before interest, tax, depreciation and amortization. It is similar to pre-tax net operating income. A multiple of EBITDA less debt is, at a high level, how venture capital values restaurants.

12 As one example from the second table above, conservative economies of scale cause Salaries & Wages to fall to 21% of revenue in the Higher Growth Revenue by year 20, which translates to a gradual 4% decrease of expenses *from this one item alone*.

right. But if you hit the top edge of those limits, it's because your business model is primed for expansion, raising the limits again.[13]

Revenue growth rate is the *only* math that can really alter the course of your business, your life and the lives of all of your team members, but you don't spend nearly enough time on it.[14] And, its probable impact is actually larger than stated because when you have a higher revenue growth rate than those of competitors, it means you also have more resources every year to out-invest to build even higher revenue and income. On the flip side, if you have a lower revenue growth rate, it means you have comparatively less to reinvest and it accelerates the decline of your rate of growth and of your income. In a nutshell:

> **Insight #14: A higher growth rate begets an even higher growth rate in a *virtuous* cycle of income growth, while a lower growth rate begets an even lower growth rate in a *vicious* cycle of income decline.**

Few restaurants ever enter the virtuous cycle of income growth, but that is precisely what this book will teach you how to do.[15] Rather, most remain in a marginal income state at risk of circumstances changing for the negative.

That is why I say that there is a brutal reality underlying the successful reduction of $600K of expense over twenty years if,

---

13 Keeping with the example of Thomas Keller, his Napa Valley model was primed for expansion (meaning it was firing on all of the principles herein) and so he was ready to develop Per Se in NYC.

14 Since the path to higher rates of growth revenue is confusing, you probably spend more time on areas where you feel more in control but that ultimately don't produce the financial outcomes you want.

15 Category leaders are the only ones who have proven capable of remaining within this virtuous cycle through thick and thin, which is how they became leaders in the first place. Every down cycle exposes businesses that look great in good times, but whose underlying model is not primed to outpace in bad times. This is why you see a shifting of leaders in disruptive periods.

during that time, your revenue growth rate underperforms those of competitors. Under this scenario, you will still likely fall into a vicious cycle of *relative* income decline as faster-growing competitors build more resources to invest to become ever-better at taking your market share.

In practice, the *vicious* cycle can play itself out over years. There are countless marginally performing restaurants that, through creative expense and cash management can keep their doors open for a long time, but they still remain slowly, perhaps imperceptibly, downward-trending businesses. Restaurants like these can trick themselves into thinking the market will improve and they will get back to achieving their start-up goals. If that is you, don't let an improving market make you believe that you now entirely control your outcomes. You still need the tools and knowledge of growth or you will continue to operate below your income potential and remain vulnerable to cycle downshifting.

Remember that it's *not* how much you are growing that matters most. What does is how much faster or slower you are growing than competitors. I have seen too often where somebody was happy with growth driven by a positive market or by the fact that they recently opened, but it didn't reflect how competitive they were. What matters is *whose competitive offer* creates superior cash flow every year to re-invest to take an ever-greater share of the pool of revenue in your market. If I could tattoo that on your arm, I would—it's that important.

Now, let's look at valuation and financing:

Valuations for privately held restaurants range widely between 0X and 8X EBITDA plus cash-on-hand, less debt and net payables. EBITDA multiples are negotiated between buyer and seller or investor and investee based on how each party forecasts the specific restaurant's future cash flows.

The *vast majority* (at least 90% in my experience) of independent restaurants would be valued by credible buyers based on multiples of 1-3 times EBITDA.[16] This is because most can't show a high probability that future income will materially increase over time. On the other hand, every year a handful of small restaurant groups or chains are valued at up to 8X EBITDA by private equity because they *can* show high future same store cash flow growth plus have proven the potential of adding new cash flows from the addition of new stores.

For analysis, let's conservatively assume that our Higher Growth Restaurant would merit a 6X EBITDA multiple while our Base Case Restaurant would only merit a 3X EBITDA (conservative because the first is at the low of the high range, and the second at the high of the low range, meaning that in other cases the valuation gap would be higher). Let's also assume that neither has debt nor material payables nor cash on hand. Under this scenario, their valuations year-by-year would look as follows:

VALUATIONS BY YEAR			
YEAR OF OPERATION	GROWTH @6X EBITDA	BASE CASE @3X EBITDA	VARIANCE BY YEAR
5	$ 621,809	$ 214,084	$ 407,725
10	$ 1,110,878	$ 260,466	$ 850,412
15	$ 1,877,576	$ 316,897	$ 1,560,679
20	$ 2,289,871	$ 385,553	$ 1,904,317

Source: Peter LeSar

If our Higher Growth Restaurant would sell to exit or use the value of its business to raise debt or equity, its valuation would be almost $2 million higher after twenty years. If your company has many units, do the math. In both cases, what would that increased valuation do for for the lives of those who rely on your business? You want and need to be the Higher Growth

16 Yes, many restaurants are worth virtually nothing, which is why so many who do sell end up financing a portion or the majority of the price. Buyers sometimes pay higher multiples on the belief they can increase future cash flow based on their own talents and not based on the cash flows locked into place at the time of sale.

Restaurant and not the Base Case,[17] which again means that you need to focus on the restaurant math that matters most: *revenue growth rates that are consistently higher than those of your competitors*. Please never forget this truth.

OBSTACLES THAT HOLD YOU BACK

From the above, we can extract three interconnected challenges in your restaurant business that suppress your revenues:

1. *You aren't performing your core job to your potential*: Your core three-part job is: A) Protect your relationships with loyal customers; B) Build back diminishing customers; and C) Add new customers at faster rates than your competitors do. If you can't do all three better than your competitors, you practically assure your eventual status as our Base Case Restaurant with all of the downside risks of that position.
2. *You don't cater to the different needs of your three customer types*: The different needs of our three customer types are: A) NCs and DCs need you to offer novelty at greater levels than competitors do in order to capture their *excitement* in a world that is inundated with commercial noise; and B) To convert and then sustain your LCs long term, they need you to keep them *interested* by solving needs that they have better than others do. The lens through which you develop quarter-to-quarter does not enable you to maximize both NC and DC excitement and LC interest at the same time, weakening your ability to drive strong demand from all three as is

[17] To spend more time on my research, I sold my two restaurants in 2018 at a valuation of more than 6X EBITDA. That was the value to me personally of deploying the lessons now written out in this book.

required to continually outperform competitors for the long term.[18]

3. *The market is more fluid than you are, meaning you can't evolve fast enough to rise up*: Competitors are progressing. New types of competition are taking revenue away from restaurants. Technology is accelerating. Your market is ever-changing and the needs of its consumers are always evolving. Macro events such as inflation, a recession and a new AI-driven world can shift behaviors almost overnight. It can be hard for any restaurant to stay ahead of all of these changes and to figure out how to rise up at the same time. It's just too much work unless, as category leaders do, you know how to multiply growth from the same or even less energy expended. My experience: Even the smallest restaurant with a single owner doing much of the work can become the most innovative leader and the newly fastest growing restaurant in a market. It's initially about prioritizing the right practice and only later about resources as you will see.

If you don't believe me on this last note, search online for the very first Chipotle and Chick-fil-A restaurants when they had almost no resources. Or, look at the original Momofuku Noodle Bar, Taco Bell or the early Joe's Stone Crab. These were *all* humble places that made it by first accepting that the Diminishing Principle is real, and second by then changing how they innovated, how often they innovated and how they exposed their innovations to the market. The Diminishing Principle is your

[18] Example: McDonald's offers novel products (Happy Meals, chicken sandwiches), ways of ordering (kiosks) and experiences (play areas, McCafé) to *excite* diminished customers and new customers to try them out. McDonald's offers value pricing to speak to the financial needs of its customers, and this sustains their *interest*. Customer excitement and interest are core to your growth model and financial outperformance; as such, we will spend a lot of time on both in this book so that you see how to build and optimize them for your restaurant.

starting point, regardless of where you are, what sort of market you are in, who you compete with and whether or not you are doing great today or less than ideal.

THE DIMINISHING PRINCIPLE

Drum roll please...

I told you at the beginning of the chapter that Thomas Keller, founder of The French Laundry, limits the number of bites in each dish he serves so that before a customer's enjoyment in a dish diminishes, she receives a new novel plate that prolongs her enjoyment of the experience as a whole.

Well guess what? Keller's approach in menu planning is conceptually similar to how you build the NC+LC-DC net balance in favor of higher growth rates. Remember that your restaurant is somewhere on these curves today:[19]

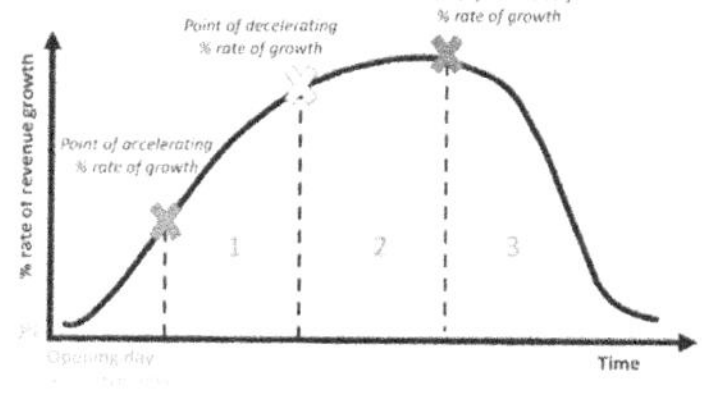

REVENUE GROWTH CURVE (DOLLAR TERMS)

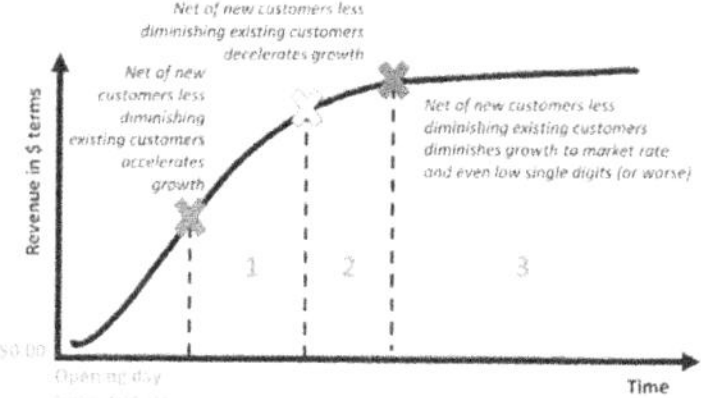

Restaurant category leaders are also on those curves. Their challenge is yours: How to avoid the eventual flattening of their revenue growth rates to uncompetitive levels once the initial novelty of their restaurants diminishes.

---

19 Reminder: The growth *rate* curve on the left inevitably pushes your growth rate down toward the market rate as existing customers diminish their interest (losing or never forming habit) and as new customers and the market diminishes its interest in you (meaning less media, less buzz, perceived less novelty). The result is that your revenue in currency terms inevitably flattens as per the chart to the right.

As you will see in the upcoming table, what they do to beat that challenge is to *build many successive growth curves by innovating frequently and deeply* to excite the market again and again—just as Keller extends excitement for his meals by pacing out one extremely novel small plate of food successively after another. Remember that initial excitement versus ongoing interest are two different processes, and your ability to re-excite the market time and again is required to attract far more NCs to try you out and far more DCs to try you again.

Whole iterative innovation jumps rather than small tactical twists (which is all that most restaurants achieve) are what recapture the market's excitement and what sustain a restaurant's momentum. Your challenge is in coming up with those innovations in any combination of products, service, ambiance, marketing, business model, distribution, expansions and so on that are impactful enough and frequent enough to generate many successive, momentum-building growth curves. What most restaurants do is that they open a static concept and then set about improving their food and service quality within that static frame. Category leaders innovate away from *where their concept starts toward a far differentiated future* as you will learn how to do in this book—It's easier to do this than you think.

> **Insight #15: Category leaders *all* follow the same innovation and growth framework because it promotes the highest, most enduring revenue growth rates.**

On the other hand:

> **Insight #16: The bottom 97% of restaurants do not know this innovation and growth framework and/or ignore the principles of outperformance that underlie it.**

The great differentiator is having the principles and framework for enduring high rates of revenue growth in place—that are simple and repeatable for you. This framework is agnostic in that it works for any restaurant of any segment located anywhere. I know because my own clients and the category leaders that I have studied are as diverse a group as you can find on this planet, and the framework works for every one of them.

On the following horizontal page is this high-level framework that I call the Restaurant Growth Model™. The result of deploying the model is to optimize two-way market discovery, meaning to: A) Help your company to continually rediscover what the market truly wants and needs; and B) Facilitate greater new customer attraction and more efficient loyal customer conversion. To really understand the Restaurant Growth Model will require that you gain more insights, which is where we are heading. Regardless, please review it carefully. Start with Step 1 at the bottom, proceed on to Step 1 (continued) at the top right, and then finally move to Step 2 and the Reinforcing Note. Then read the explanation and short cases further below.

RESTAURANT GROWTH MODEL™ [20]

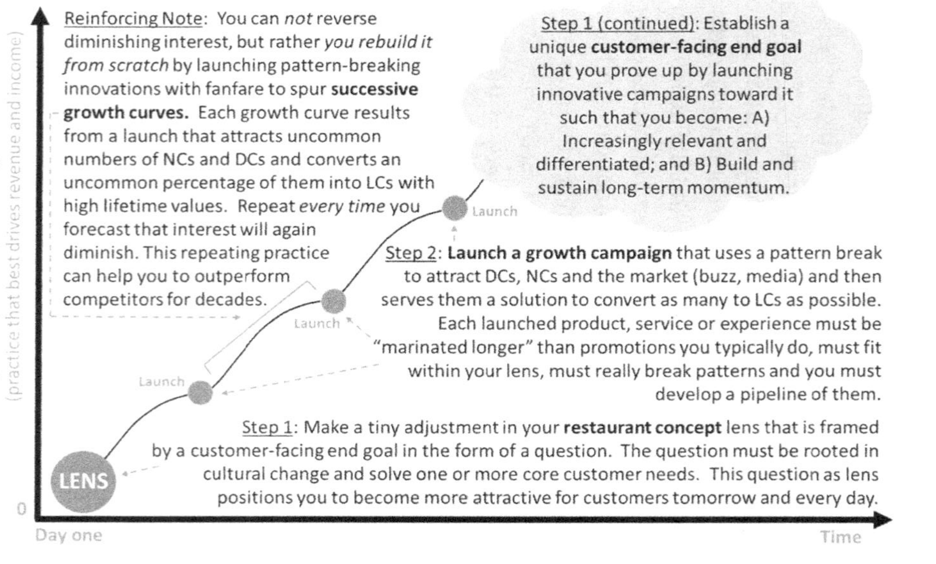

Source: Peter LeSar

20 I suggest you print this diagram and keep it with you as you read the book. It will help you to place what you read into an overall approach to growth. It can be found at www.DineRock.com

Restaurants that emerge as category leaders don't drift, but rather navigate:

- Step 1 and Step 1 (continued) jointly act as a *compass* that points to a game-changing, customer-facing direction that nobody has led in before. In combination, the two parts of Step 1 gift you the beginning and end of a navigation route. When you travel restaurant ground already well tread by others, somebody else has solved the problems ahead of you. There is emotional comfort for you in having existing models to follow, but not financial comfort of the type to which you aspire. *It is in walking on new ground toward a solution for customers that nobody has built before that greatness and great financial outcomes are earned in our business.*
- Step 2 is how you repeatedly *reignite excitement* from NCs and DCs and convert them at higher and higher rates to LCs. The Step 2 practice raises your rate of new customer acquisition, reduces your rate of diminishing customers, and drives up your conversion of both to loyal customers. Revenue and income lift as you forever stack up more loyal customers and their lifetime values. *Most restaurants never learn the deep practice of continuing high rates of same store growth, which is what has most driven the outperformance of category leaders. This book lays it all out for you.*

All First Principles of Revenue & Income Outperformance that you will learn herein are integrated into this framework such that, at the end of the book, you should be able to look at the Restaurant Growth Model diagram and understand deeply each of your successive growth moves.

This is going to get exciting.

Case in point. After Noma had won the top spot (for the fourth time) on the list of The World's 50 Best Restaurants™, it just couldn't raise market interest any higher than that. It risked diminishing interest. Noma's answer: shut down, go on the road to cook in Japan, Australia and Mexico, look through its customer-facing lens and launch newly novel Noma 2.0 that *reignited* excitement from all over the globe as it increased its opportunities for innovation to attract a greater number of NCs and DCs, and for solving human needs to convert a higher percentage of LCs. As you will learn, Noma's process of developing, timing and acting reflected the Restaurant Growth Model in action and led to it regaining the World's Best Restaurant title.

After Starbucks had absorbed much of the growth out of the market, in 2006 Dunkin' Donuts made a tiny adjustment in its concept, which opened up new innovation paths that increased NC acquisitions, convinced DCs to return and converted more of both to long-term LCs. The result: Dunkin's growth shot up from 7,000 stores in 2006 (that took 58 years to develop) to over 14,000 stores today. As you will see in depth, Dunkin's process of developing, timing and acting also reflected the Restaurant Growth Model in action.

The Restaurant Growth Model will start to unfold in the next chapter. We will begin by discussing **how your restaurant concept slipped off track** and how you can reset it to build your company's greatest future.

CHAPTER 2

A PRIORI TRUTH PRINCIPLE

How to tweak your restaurant concept into a game-changing one.

I STOOD IN A SHADOWED corner of one of our restaurants watching the floor at peak dinner hours. The day before, I had returned to Asia from a tough shareholders' meeting in Zurich. I was anxious to check in on the business. The dinner service that evening flowed beautifully as our team connected to each other, to our guests and to what was needed in every interaction. It was like a dance. We had step-by-step become operationally competitive. I remember thinking "our customers in Asia look happier than our shareholders in Zurich." Financially the business was still off and this made me wonder: *Is it common for a restaurant to operate at a high level and yet underperform as a business?*

Since this question first came to me years ago, I have spoken with hundreds of owners, chefs and executives who work hard to eliminate customer frustrations and to serve them as many happy moments as possible. Most share a hard reality: It *is* common for restaurants to produce moderate financial outcomes even when they offer great service and food.

This realization led me to a follow-on question: *Why are customers attracted in droves to category leaders?* We now know that it isn't necessarily their operations that draw crowds as many restaurants that operate at high levels don't have their same traffic. We can also infer that food quality and flavor isn't the reason either, because when you compare category leaders from the likes of Subway to Olive Garden to 11 Madison Park, you realize that quality and flavor exist in a broad, subjective continuum and offer no universal explanations of success.[21] My job is to find what is universal in our business so that you can rely on it, and not to call out a hundred different explanations of success for a hundred different cases. That doesn't serve your interest. So, what is that universal magic fairy dust that category leaders have mastered, but that most restaurant concepts overlook entirely? This chapter responds to that question by answering another:

How do you adjust your restaurant concept to excite the market for even decades?

In other words, how do we *bridge the knowledge gap* between having:

A SO-SO CONCEPT ·········➜ A GAME-CHANGING CONCEPT

Amazingly, there is a single source, a seed if you will, that excites extraordinary interest in restaurants. Any restaurant from any market can plant or test that seed to increase demand for its offerings. This chapter speaks to how to adjust your concept to make it ever-more *exciting to an ever-broadening customer base.*

---

21 High standards of operational performance do differentiate, for example, the destination fine dining segment from local fine dining. Within segments, however, the standards are raised at a similar pace—meaning virtually all fast casual leaders (as one segment example) maintain service and food quality metrics within a range that is largely imperceptible to the general public. The point: Operational excellence and food quality *are absolutely critical*, but so many restaurants are raising their standards continuously that high standards of performance are now a baseline requirement just to remain competitive within your segment.

WHAT WE NOTICE ARE PATTERN BREAKS

Think for a moment about everything that fights for your attention in a typical day. We all exist in permanent sensory overload. Experts estimate that we filter through thousands of messages and pieces of content a day, and AI is only speeding this up. News on all sides promotes controversy to steal away our attention. We see, hear, taste, smell and touch in all of our waking hours. While asleep, we dream stories and continue to use our physical senses. Our senses are overwhelmed 24/7 by far more than we can possibly assimilate. So, let's start with a simple question: *With so much going on in your life around the clock, what causes you personally to notice something?*

If there is coffee brewing in a fresh morning kitchen, you smell it. When a red balloon flies past a blue sky, you see it. When a baby cries in a quiet restaurant or a priest swears in church, you notice it. Which *single* factor in each of these scenes causes you to pause and take note?

> **Insight #17: When something surprisingly contrasts against a normally consistent backdrop, what we notice is the *juxtaposition* between the two.**

If thirty babies were crying and a new cry joined in, you wouldn't hear it. If a hundred red balloons flew past, you wouldn't see the next one. What we notice is not any specific sensory input, but rather when there are sharp contrasts. And, the sharper the contrast, the more we notice. Restaurants use juxtaposition all of the time to capture our attention:

- A colorful entrée plated on a large white dish.
- McDonald's golden arches raised against a blue sky.
- Three-dimensional cow bill boards vs. a world of two-dimensional signs.

When there are stark contrasts, our ancient biology takes note.[22] To eat, our ancestors needed to be able to spot the curved horns of a gazelle hidden within the swaying grass. To avoid being eaten, they needed to be able to discern the movement of a python and the roar of a tiger against a forest backdrop.

Repetitive patterns such as grass lands for our ancestors and strip malls for us today dull our senses. Repetitive patterns are our reference points of what is normal and safe and therefore our brains learn to ignore them, freeing up energy and mind space for the *pattern breaks* that alert us to potential opportunities and dangers. This is critical because:

> **Insight 18: Restaurants become category leaders only after they make a sharp enough break from restaurant patterns that we notice the juxtaposition.**

Steve Ells, founder of Chipotle, in his early days wouldn't waste time telling everyone how delicious their burritos were. That is the expected pattern of how restaurants act, and doesn't work well. Rather, he would speak to what was then a revolutionary pattern break that juxtaposed against industry patterns:

"The traditional fast-food model is built on buying the cheapest ingredients - and that usually means poor-quality,

[22] From now on, when you see green parsley next to a blandly colored meal or a green olive in a clear martini or a logo with no name (i.e., golden arches or the mythological Starbuck's siren), please recall that juxtaposition is at the center of how we stand out. In fact, juxtaposition stems from our pre-human evolution. Unlike other mammals, the monkeys from whom we evolved developed color sightedness that enabled them to spot orange, yellow and red fruit among a dense green forest canopy. Symbiotically, fruit adapted into colors that best juxtaposed against that canopy so that monkeys would find the fruit, eat it and disperse its seeds. While there are numerous research papers and sources on the evolution of the food humans eat, a particularly great resource is the book *Tasty: The Art and Science of What We Eat* written by Pulitzer Prize-winning author John McQuaid.

heavily processed foods. But you can use quality ingredients, cook food using classic cooking techniques, and still serve something that's fast and inexpensive."[vii]

Your restaurant's juxtaposition must be sharp in both how you describe it *and* how you practice it. I still remember the first time I went to Chipotle. The blended décor of birchwood, corrugated metal and polished cement juxtaposed to the then normal fast-food environment of plastic furniture and institutional beige-tiled floors. Servers prepared my food in front of me and from fresh ingredients as a pattern break to fast food where processed meals were assembled out of view. My burrito was wrapped in foil as a pattern break to fast food styrofoam. For those who don't remember a world before fast casual, these juxtapositions were so powerful that every customer and journalist who visited a Chipotle took note and talked about them.

Insight #19: Sharp juxtaposition drives how often and how passionately people talk about you. To drive conversations and media, restaurants must break established patterns.

Think about the reference points you have broken. Can you point to any? If so, are they strong and clear enough of a break from common restaurant patterns that your whole market takes note? Most likely not and therefore prospective customers' thoughts and conversations go to others that do and you lose revenue and income as a result. Breaking patterns to the extent required to get noticed and to sustain being noticed is hard unless you know where to start.

It is further complicated by the passage of *time* and by the *frequency* with which people encounter you. If gazelles were to hide among the tall grass all day, every day, we would no longer notice them either. When they too join the pattern, they no longer break it. Likewise, when we have seen countless Chick-fil-A billboards in our lives, though still pattern breaking, we no longer notice them. Our senses are dulled by the passage of time and by the frequency with which we encounter something.

This raises a slightly different question: *When something has lost its former pattern-breaking shine, when do we notice it again?* If a priest swears every day in church, we would learn to ignore it. But if he were to strip tease one day, we would notice his new odd behavior. In other words:

> **Insight #20: When something loses its shine of novelty and becomes common place, for us to notice, it must *again* show us something surprisingly different.**

McDonald's perfected the assembly line kitchen and we noticed the *juxtaposition* of its speedy service and discount pricing to all of the inefficient hamburger grills it competed against. Buzz and excitement followed McDonald's everywhere until we had experienced these advantages often enough that they became commonplace and no longer surprisingly different. McDonald's later introduced Happy Meals with toys, indoor playgrounds, combo meals (that were even cheaper per unit of food), a clown named Ronald McDonald, kiosks for ordering and so on, all that were intentionally designed to juxtapose to restaurants of those the times so that we would notice and pay heed time and again.

Learning to spot and sharply break product, service, experience and marketing patterns is a growth multiplier that is core to the Restaurant Growth Model (look at the model again with fresh eyes). You will see how to do this in Chapter 5. If you can't juxtapose yourself from the patterns that people experience in their everyday lives, and then do it again and again, you will fail to be noticed to the extent required to drive extraordinary financial outcomes. Without such an approach, you essentially guarantee that you will just be one more gazelle among thousands. Pretty. Graceful perhaps. But blended in among all except for those few restaurants that are like tiger roars in a silent forest.

THE SOURCE OF GREAT OUTCOMES

When I started observing category leaders more closely, I noticed they all regularly expressed big, original themes:

"...the food that we know in America, Black people got written out of it. We have to figure out a way to get back into it."[viii]
- Marcus Samuelsson, founder of Red Rooster and bestselling author

"Every public school...should have a nutrition-education curriculum."[ix]
- Cat Cora, founder of Cat Cora's Kitchen and Iron Chef winner

"Food is a national security issue."[x]
- Jose Andres, founder of World Central Kitchen

Original thinking about big themes is required to juxtapose yourself to competitors, because the reverse is to think about the inconsequential that leads to innovations that carry little meaning.[23] So, what *seeds* the original thinking that has helped all category leaders to emerge? To start, let's examine a statement from Noma founder Rene Redzepi:

---

[23] You might think that if you put a "twist" or your "take" on this concept or that meal that you are offering something meaningful to the public, but both imply low levels of contrast. You need to think in starker terms as juxtaposition is about opposites and not about 2.1 to 2.2 level iterations. Examples of sharp juxtaposition in restaurant concepts: a) Blue Hill at Stone Barns brought the table to the farm rather than the farm to the table as most "farm-to-table" restaurants do; b) Donde Jose (a restaurant I founded) was the most expensive restaurant in its market, but located in gang territory; and c) EveryTable, a small California chain, prices its nutritious grab-n-go meals not based on a multiple of food costs (as everyone else does as a pattern), but on the median income around each location so that healthy eating is *always* locally affordable. Sharp juxtapositions excite the media, create conversations and entice large numbers of new customers.

"Scandinavian-Danish cuisine was something quite rustic, mostly known for pastries and smorgasbord cuisine, which in itself has become a joke."

Redzepi's *first* intent with this statement was to say that there had been a "cultural truth" in Scandinavia that its cuisine should be expressed to the world through smorgasbords. Cultural truths are the *hidden-in-plain-site seeds of originality* in our business, so what are they?

A "cultural truth" is a widely held belief that things must be a certain way.

As an example, we as a culture might believe that fine dining should be served on fine china rather than on paper plates. There is no rule that fine china is an obligatory element of fine dining, but because fine china has been relied on for so long, it *feels like a rule* of how fine dining meals must be plated. Cultural truths feel like *the* rules of how we must behave as humans and operate as businesses.

Having both front-of-the-house and back-of-the-house employees (rather than re-engineering such that only BoH employees run meals) is a cultural truth.[24] Providing guests with a menu of choices in fast food (rather than offering one meal a day) is a cultural truth. So is taking a reservation for free rather than charging to hold one. Tipping is a cultural truth that Danny

---

[24] BoH employees often feel unfairly excluded from tip sharing given that they also work hard and can be more skilled than FoH teams. Here is one solution to the problem. Re-engineer operations such that your BoH runs all food directly from the kitchen to the table. Rotate all BoH through the dining floor and train them on FoH work. In most markets, these steps will be sufficient for regulators to accept that BoH share in the tip pool. This approach should make your BoH team the highest paid among your competitors and allow you to retain the best talent—lowering churn as a result. Unless you are in a fast segment, this structure should increase productivity, allow you to reduce payroll and should reduce or eliminate frictions and service break downs between FoH and BoH operations.

Meyer and others have tried breaking, and the difficulties they encountered show just how embedded cultural truths can be. Cultural truths can feel uncomfortable to question (people often shame those that do) and we often fear taking them on, but:

Insight #21: Deconstructing cultural truths is how we find original approaches and is how future category leaders emerge.

Cultural truths are so embedded in our beliefs that we usually don't see them even though they guide all behaviors in restaurants, including: The purpose of our different meals. What we think we should serve according to our restaurant concept. Décor and layouts. Our perception of good locations. What we say to guests and how we serve them. How meals are priced. Language on menus and menu design. Staffing structures and hierarchies. Uniforms. Tipping. Service levels. The way tables are set. The utensils we use. And endlessly on.

The list of cultural truths is *endless* because every single practice we accept as common in our lives is in fact a cultural truth. Cultural truths reflect repeating patterns of unwritten rules that a culture unquestioningly accepts as to how we should live, work, relate and behave in the world to get along with others. To be crystal clear: *Restaurants that break cultural truths are those that win, because they excite our attention—and yet cultural truths are everywhere and so there are many more opportunities to win than winners in our business.*

A cultural truth among some restaurants in Denmark was that to attract foreign visitors they needed to serve smorgasbords, which in 2004 when Noma opened meant abundant buffets that depended in part on imported ingredients from continental Europe. Neither the abundance nor the imported ingredients reflected the values and identity of the Danish people. Smorgasbords were a cultural truth of how the world perceived Danish eating habits, but weren't indicative of Danes' eating customs at all.[25, xi]

The *second* intent of Redzepi's statement was to suggest that it was time to write a new truth for the country's cuisine that aligned with the modern culture of the Danes themselves, and that broke the pattern of the cultural truth. That new truth was to implement and lead the New Nordic Cuisine manifesto that proposed that Nordic restaurants rely only on the scarce ingredients found in the region's "climates, landscapes and waters" rather than on an abundance of imported ingredients that had been the pattern for decades.

So, to clarify, what has seeded the extraordinary outcomes of category leaders and is needed to seed yours as well?

> **Insight #22: You must identify a widely held belief (cultural truth) and then use it to identify a *new opposite* or *highly contrarian belief*. The new belief is like a first domino that will set you up to knock down many successive**

[25] Cultural truths usually seem absurd in hindsight, but when you study the era when those truths were shaped, they made sense then. Smorgasbords are an example of this. The word "smorgasbord" translates as "a table of buttered bread" and, according to Kitchn, "its roots are found in the upper class of 14th century Sweden where a small spread of bread, butter, and cheese was offered before mealtime." So where did the cultural truth of abundant smorgasbords come from? It all started during the 1919 Olympics in Sweden "when smorgasbords grew to include meats, both hot and cold" and "officially became the main meal instead of an appetizer." Two decades later at the 1939 World Fair in New York City, the Swedish Pavilion set up a smorgasbord as a buffet meal that celebrated abundance and the good life. America fell in love and this single smorgasbord helped spark the eventual craze for American buffets (that were further popularized in Las Vegas casinos). Over time, visitors to Scandinavia sought out this style of abundant smorgasbord and restaurants in Denmark adjusted to cater to the demand. In summary: The cultural truth that Danish restaurants should serve abundant smorgasbords evolved out of events on foreign lands, was constructed as an attraction for visitors, but was never rooted as Danish custom.

patterns over time—all only discoverable because of the first one.

You can't spot a way to break a pattern if you don't first see the pattern itself. Cultural truths are those patterns in life that blend into the background, while your breaking from one with a new truth and the physical manifestations of that truth are the tiger roars that people notice. Sometimes pattern breaks can even produce monumental leaps forward because:

Insight #23: Cultural truths as reference points can help us to spot systemic weaknesses that inspire *next step innovations* in how we live and operate.

Fire was our first cooking reference point approximately 250,000 years ago, and led us to develop primitive ways of skewering meat. Skewers used on open fires allowed heat to escape, and were our reference point for building containers of clay, wood, antlers and bones so that we could slow cook meals. Early success at containing heat was the reference point for developing tightly enclosed ovens around 4500 B.C. And so on it continues through today and for all of human history to come. The culture in each era of humankind (including ours) believes that the techniques of their time reflect the best patterns—until all of a sudden somebody breaks a pattern and a new form of sourcing or cooking or serving or doing emerges.

When you recognize that all behaviors are cultural truths and that all cultural truths are reference points that show us what might be changed, you open up the possibility that you can uncover a next stage of restaurant practice that nobody has yet focused on. Again, the rule of thumb: break patterns to win *or* follow the patterns and don't. As you can see from the above:

Insight #24: Some cultural truths endure for a generation and some for much longer.

> **The more embedded a cultural truth, the *more valuable it is* to break with a new truth aligned to where your culture is heading in the coming years.**[26]

Cultural truths are simply patterns that, in breaking them, offer outsized opportunities. If you break a product pattern by changing up the bun of a hamburger, then that is a smaller growth opportunity. If you break a cultural truth by changing how a market behaves, then that is potentially a huge growth opportunity. Smorgasbords were a valuable cultural truth to break because they were embedded in local practices for so long that breaking from them required that tourists, local foodies and local restaurants reset their expectations and behaviors. When Redzepi made the statement about smorgasbords, he was telling us that the generations' old reference point should no longer speak for Denmark's modern, progressive identity. Scandinavian-Danish cuisine, Redzepi proclaimed, had "become a joke" and the cultural truth needed to be forever broken.

Redzepi in that one statement gave evidence to something critical: Replacing a cultural truth with a new opposite or highly contrarian new truth is your *first step* to exciting a market by catalyzing change to a level that most never achieve.

HOW TO FIND YOUR MOST VALUABLE CONCEPT

Let's understand foremost that restaurants are an expression of where a culture is in its development. A *class* of restaurants that is fading or expanding signals that what a culture values is in flux. Since there is always at least one class of restaurant trending up in demand and one trending down, you know that your culture is in fact in constant transition.

[26] To paraphrase hockey legend Wayne Gretzky: "A good *restaurant* plays where *culture* is. A great *restaurant* plays where *culture* is going to be."

In the United States from the early 2000s through today, fast casual revenue growth has outpaced that of fast food because the former expresses an emerging consensus that we should consume real ingredients over processed ones. In the same time period, casual dining struggled as American culture required more speed (as it found in fast casual) or greater levels of service and experience (as it did in casual fine). The middle ground that is casual dining was the once *seemingly indomitable* pattern that we lost interest in as our values changed.

Imagine a cliff a thousand feet high and a hundred miles long. That seemingly indomitable wall is your culture and it is constantly crashed against and slowly eroded by waves of new influences. Those new influences come from our own travels, from immigrants, advancing technology, from new levels of understanding about any wide range of ideas (nutrition, environment, community, justice, religion and so on), democratization of information and from marginalized populations that are newly empowered to express their own beliefs.

Most of us see the huge cliff of steadfast culture, but what matters most for the future of restaurants are those waves of new influences knocking against the status quo. New influences are forebearers of old trends that are fading and losing value and of large opportunities to come. Like this one was:

> *New York City bars in 1965 were dark, smoky and deemed by the culture of the time to be inappropriate for women to visit. One way for single men and women to meet up in the early 1960s was to go to a cocktail party at somebody's home. First-time restaurateur Allan Stillman bought a bar, merged it with the concept of a cocktail party in a way that was attractive and safe-feeling for women, and gave birth to the original singles' bar where singles were now excited to meet at night outside of the home. Stillman road the cultural curve of a women's*

movement and the liberalizing of nightlife in America. He called his place TGI Friday's, the first singles bar positioned on the wave crest of the sexual revolution.[27]

What most don't realize is that TGI Friday's became a global icon, better known internationally than the much larger Applebee's and other American casual family dining chains. Why is that? Because it brought its new truth of a fun (but safe) singles bar to countries that were also experiencing their own waves of sexual and nightlife liberation. TGI Friday's led its part of the cultural change and, symbiotically, the cultural change created great demand for TGI Friday's offerings.

Insight #25: *Leading cultural change* creates our biggest opportunities and there is usually one leader who benefits far more than the rest. Following cultural change offers only crumbs of income to share as many copycat competitors pile on only after a trend is full blown.

It's not just Noma and TGI Friday's that have benefited immensely from leading cultural change. Ferran Adrià's El Bulli pioneered the deconstructivism movement of breaking traditional recipes down to their culinary essence and rebuilding them into

---

27 TGI Friday's made a strategy turn after Stillman sold it to a private equity group. Even though it thrived as a single's bar in urban areas, its investors were tempted by the growing suburban markets of the 70s and 80s. They expanded the brand into the suburban family dining segment, but each unit continued to offer a singles' environment in its bar area. TGI Friday's move diluted its ability to become the strongest competitor for either market. Specifically, it lost its opportunity to build a global leader in the singles' bar category. Since just prior to Covid-19, TGI Friday's has returned to the singles' bar concept as its core development focus, but this point of view is now outdated and management has struggled to uncover a new point of view for changing times. Restaurant Strong (and DineRock) helps to solve for this challenge of outdated positioning, which challenge suppresses the growth potential of most restaurant companies.

pattern-breaking forms that the global gastro-tourist culture now expects from destination fine dining. Christina Tosi's Milk Bar led the neo-nostalgic movement of elevating undervalued desserts from our past, and others than followed. Jeremiah Tower's Stars led the redefinition of restaurants from only dining to entertainment-dining experiences. None of these restaurants followed the change nor focused foremost on the tactical curves of our industry. All of them *led the cultural curve of history* by rewriting the truths of their time to spark or ride the cresting transformation of the restaurant experience before the rest of us even discerned a new wave shaping.[28]

HOW TO OWN TOP OF MIND

As I expanded my research into how category leaders emerge, I noticed something important that is related to the discussion above but that requires a special focus:

- Noma made the world *rethink* Nordic cuisine.
- Chick-fil-A made us *rethink* that business and religious principles can work together to inspire a tribe of fans and extraordinary financial outcomes.
- SweetGreen is making us *think* that food served fast can actually be both tasty and nutritious for us.

In a nutshell:

Insight #26: The most successful restaurants change how humanity *thinks*.

---

[28] Most of us see trends in the news and shape our restaurants to ride trends that already have leaders. Leaders find new truths inflecting on the periphery of culture that they can lead before others even notice them. Agility Capital and DineRock help portfolio companies and advisory clients to develop well ahead of trends, which is part of every category leader's critical path to upshifting income trajectories.

In a great *Financial Times* interview, when Howard Schultz of Starbucks says...

"It's about the humanity."

...he is saying that humans connect with brands for reasons beyond product. The more a company makes us think about new ideas they bring to the forefront, the more we think about a company. The more Schultz talked about the need for a third place[29]—where coffee can "bring people together"—and the more he manifested that best third place with innovations, the more we collectively thought, wrote and talked about Starbucks. Convincing a culture to rethink what it needs and how it lives is what earns the most valuable of real estate: *our top of mind*.

A restaurant thrives when customers *recall* it quickly above all competitors. Food and service quality alone do *not* optimize recall for anyone beyond your loyal customers, and that is why focusing exclusively on them doesn't produce the growth you want. Remember the formula:

RG *(revenue growth)* = NCs (new customer spending) + LCs (loyal customer spending) – DC (lost consumption from *diminishing customers*)

Your job is to increase your rate of new customer acquisition, which means that you need consumers who are *not* showing up to recall you, but that requires you to be on the top of mind of an entire market rather than just on top of mind of already loyal customers—most restaurant professionals never see that and therefore never learn to solve for it. So, how do you train an entire market to recall you? The book "Play Bigger, How Pirates,

[29] For those unfamiliar with the "third place" concept, Schultz wanted to create a venue that was a third place that people might want to hang out in (to socialize, work, study and just relax) that was neither their home nor their office. This was a radical idea then in the United States (outside of bars), though was already a reality in Italy's espresso bars and in European cafes in general.

Dreamers and Innovators Create Categories and Dominate Markets", wonderfully describes the relationship between changing how humanity thinks and category leadership:

> *"Your number one job is to change the way people think. Your product, your company culture, your marketing—everything has to be aligned with transforming the way potential customers think. If you change the way they think, they will change their buying behavior. More important, if you are the company that changes the way people think, people will see your company as the category king, and you will win the majority of the customers."*[xii]

Flipping a cultural truth on its head is the epitome of getting us to rethink, but you have some choices on how to do this:

- You can specialize in short-term *tactical* splashes that are surprisingly different but don't make us rethink anything for long .[30] Taco Bell does this successfully with crazy inventive menu items that it launches on a schedule to continually renew growth.[31] I refer to this level of

---

30 Examples of restaurants that build demand by breaking tactical cultural truths: Le Refuge de Fondu in Paris has driven decades of high traffic counts by questioning why we can't drink wine in baby bottles (new truth) rather than wine glasses (cultural truth). Vinnie's Pizzeria in Brooklyn has created global press and huge demand by questioning why the Pizza delivery box can't be made of edible crust (new truth) rather than cardboard (cultural truth). Alinea in Chicago has used molecular gastronomy to flip tactical cultural truths with its transparent pumpkin pie (why does pie need to always look the same). Ithaa in the Maldives questions why you can't eat underwater. Dinner in the Sky questions why we can't eat at the top of a crane. El Diablo in Spain questions why we can't cook over a live volcano. Sur un Arbre Perche in France questions why we need chairs or booths, when we could dine in swings. Examples of tactical rethinking that increase revenues are endless, but usually they are less valuable and scalable than flipping cultural truths around human values.

31 Items such as Nacho Cheese Doritos®, Locos Tacos Supreme®, Grilled Cheese Burrito and Crunchwrap Supreme®.

cultural truth breaking as simple "pattern breaks", and anyone can do them with a little practice and a shift in how they observe the patterns that they and competitors fall into (as further discussed in Chapter 5).

- Or, you can break cultural truths that are based on *values* and build top of mind that can last even beyond your own lifetime. Chez Panisse will *always* be on American culture's top of mind when we discuss farm to table, and can never be knocked down by a competitor – you can't out invest a restaurant that is synonymous with making us rethink our values to such an extent that it will forever be more *recallable*. We will work on this value level of cultural truth breaking at the end of this chapter.[32]
- You can also do both. You can use the lens of your new truth to find tactical innovations that surprise people *and* that deepen the dialogue around the values you are leading in. SweetGreen has done this with its Outpost program that delivers one-to-many (rather than one-to-one meal delivery) for buildings that love its values, and with a network of local producers that collectively compete with the offerings of the large distributors.

Rethinking equals recalling. Recalling equals revenue. The more profound the rethink that you can bring to the world and the more frequently you can get us to rethink, the greater the recall and the more enduring your rate of revenue growth. It is literally that simple, but how do you make it happen? Before answering that question, let's look at what stands in your way.

[32] To be clear in the Taco Bell example, it chose to break a cultural truth around values that showed it many of the tactical patterns that it broke thereafter. You will see a case study on this later.

OBSTACLES THAT HOLD YOU BACK

Our restaurants were operationally competitive and yet something stood in our way of exciting demand. Our growth problems began the day we opened an incomplete concept, which caused knock-on challenges as you will see. Here are those *concept* challenges faced by us, by you and by most restaurants that shortchange all of our abilities to excite the market:

1. *Your restaurant concept is incomplete*: You started your business by making tactical decisions (product, service level, location, etc.) in lieu of first defining how you wanted to influence your market or the world. When you form your concept through a tactical lens first, it's virtually impossible to differentiate yourself *enough* that customers understand the stark, contrasting value you offer. This is a recipe for a growth trajectory that is similar to that of the majority of the market, meaning that you are not positioned to sustain outperforming rates of revenue and income growth long term. So, how do you adjust your concept such that it excites the market even many years after most restaurants would have long since matured?
2. *Your concept was not conceived as an "a priori truth"*: Before all other truths is "a priori truth", which means a truth found before there is evidence of its viability. For example, an a priori truth of mine was that in researching category leaders, I could find first principles of how restaurants rise. There was no evidence that this was the case, which meant I gifted myself the *opportunity to break new ground.* Redzepi's a priori truth was that he could pioneer a new cuisine by sourcing exclusively in ingredient-scarce arctic and sub-arctic environments. He gifted Noma the opportunity to break new ground. Your restaurant has not reached its potential because it was formed from "a posteriori knowledge", meaning a similar or the same concept has worked elsewhere and

others have already broken the ground in that space. A posteriori knowledge is a safe zone where growth potential is low because it does not gift you the *surprisingly different* pattern breaks on to new ground that excite customers and media. If Redzepi had decided to rely on imported ingredients as most Danish restaurants did at the time, Noma would have missed all of the pattern breaks it uncovered. Pattern breaks are like dominos—knock down the first one and other pattern break opportunities emerge naturally. On the other hand, when you work in the realm of a posteriori knowledge it's hard to see the patterns that you live in, let alone break any. You need to adjust out of this low-growth zone to a higher one, but you don't know how.

The above challenges cause additional pain as follows:

- If you are *emotionally disconnected from your concept*, it's because it doesn't offer you the opportunity to be the first creator of something. Bringing a new idea to life is how many find purpose, but it must be truly new to open the paths for innovation that sustain and build purpose.
- If you find it *hard to create novelty that resonates*, it's because to do so is almost impossible unless you start from a different place than everyone (an a priori truth that breaks a cultural truth is the level of "different place" required to start new innovation paths from).
- If your *income doesn't match that of your start-up dreams*, it's because demand grows proportionally to how frequently a broadening market recalls you, and your concept doesn't give *more* people *more* to think about as compared to competitors (the relative comparison is what counts). Rather the market thinks about you infrequently even though you poke at it with social media and in other common ways, following the tactical curve of others that never actually leads to where you want to go.

The A Priori Truth Principle sweeps these challenges away.

A PRIORI TRUTH PRINCIPLE

The A Priori Truth Principle responds to our need to excite the market to look at us again and again as it does with category leaders. The A Priori Truth Principle contends that:

> *Most restaurant concepts have three missing links that, when absent, reduce income potential. We will discuss the first two missing links now, and the third one in the next chapter. The first missing link is defining a cultural truth to break. The second missing link is identifying an a priori truth born out of that cultural truth, meaning a new truth that has never been proven before, but that seems self-evident once you examine it deeply. As discussed, for your concept to generate extraordinary outcomes requires that it excite the market even for decades to come—proving up an a priori truth is what creates the conditions for that enduring excitement (see relevant case study below).*[33]

In a lengthy November 2004 article in the *New York Times* titled "Here Comes Ramen, The Slurp Heard Around the World" Momofuku Noodle Bar's then relatively unknown founder David Chang was granted a single quote: "New York might never have really great ramen, just like Tokyo might never have really great pizza. But I'm having a lot of fun trying."[xiii] This was Chang's tactical concept phase, when he believed that bringing a new product to market (the ramen craze was just starting in NYC) would position his restaurant for growth. As you can see from

[33] You will learn the other missing concept link in a future chapter.

his sort of empty*ish* quote,[34] in this tactical phase he wasn't a thought leader yet because tactics didn't give him interesting content to talk about. It was in this tactical concept phase when Momofuku Noodle Bar was at risk of closing for business as Chang himself has said: "We had zero money. We were straining to do this [tactical] 'noodle bar' concept, limiting ourselves in the kitchen, limiting what we could cook, and constantly hearing about 'authenticity' and how we didn't embody it."[xiv] The Momofuku Noodle Bar concept was missing something.

Just five months later, in April 2005, the *New York Times* published an article that opened with: "GOOD restaurants don't always start off at the top of their game. That's how I felt watching Momofuku Noodle Bar evolve over the last eight months from a promising underachiever into one of the East Village's best new restaurants." Chang said of this same period: "People started coming to the restaurant more often. We were full a lot. After a while, a little crowd of people waiting outside became the norm. Insolvency wasn't as immediate a threat. All of a sudden, the press began paying an undue amount of attention to us."

What changed so dramatically in a matter of months?

This question speaks to how ordinary restaurants rise to achieve extraordinary outcomes. Chang's explanation was that "something happened" when Momofuku started "expanding the boundaries of what we served" and became "more than a shitty [tactic-led] noodle bar." The *New York Times*' explanation of Momofuku's progress was that it had come to occupy "the realm of deeply personal restaurants defined by one person's vision" and was a reflection of Chang's "background as a Korean-American chef."

I have the benefit of hindsight and of significant study of the matter and can be much more specific. What changed was that Momofuku's concept had begun its evolution from one led

---

34 I assume Chang will laugh when he reads this. No offense David:)

by low-value tactics to a concept led by two high-value a priori truths that broke two deeply embedded cultural truths:

Chang's first cultural truth and its countervailing a priori truth: As he matured, Chang hit on two very embedded cultural truths in a single restaurant. The first can be seen in Chang's 2018 interview in *GQ Magazine* when he said: "What bothers me...is the categorisation of restaurants."[xv] The cultural truth Chang identified was that restaurant professionals and customers of the time inherently believed that Asian restaurants should be siloed off as either Japanese or Korean or Thai and so on and that "American" cuisine should also be siloed to reflect only the culinary roots of American citizens descended from Europe and Africa. Chang's a priori truth is expressed in *Momofuku: A Cookbook* when he wrote of his desire to "serve delicious American food" in which "labne and ssämjang and Sichuan peppercorns and poached rhubarb all end up in the same kitchen." In other words, his first a priori truth was to recognize the Americanness of ethnically non-African and non-European citizens, and to incorporate all of America's culinary roots into a redefined American cuisine. While other restaurants serving Asian or American food were trapped on siloed ground living the patterns of their era, Chang's new truth freed him from that cultural truth and gifted the Noodle Bar the opportunity to break new ground. One food editor said as quoted in *GQ Magazine*: "It's delicious, but not like any other delicious."[xvi] That is exactly what pattern breaks do...they make you unlike any other.

Chang's second cultural truth and its countervailing a priori truth: The second cultural truth Chang uncovered is also expressed in *Momofuku: A Cookbook*: "Food doesn't have to be served in a fine dining setting to be good." Chang knew that even street food in Asia could be quite sophisticated (I have seen this many times myself). When the Momofuku Noodle Bar was founded, the fact that fine food in the United States was served almost exclusively in fine dining establishments was a cultural truth waiting to be broken. *Chang's second a priori truth was that fine food could be served across all formats*, which gifted him the opportunity to again break ground and introduce his new version of American fine food into Ssäm Bar[35] (cocktail bar), Ko[36] (fine counter dining), bāng bar[37] (food stall), majordōmo[38] (fine dining) and Fuku (fast casual)[39, xvii, xviii, xix, xx]

Chang's cultural and a priori truths were two of three missing links that bridged his initially marginal outcomes to extraordinary ones. They gifted him with a lens to uncover innovations in cuisine, formats and in the language of thought leadership.[40] Those innovations inspired early adopting customers to try the Noodle Bar out. Media loved his ground breaking and placed the restaurant on top of mind for its readers. The combination of early customer and media excitement exploded the number of visitors he could convert to loyal customers. Restaurants that ignore cultural truths and a priori truths are not able to duplicate this level of success. It's the fire we must walk through in order to evolve into and emerge as category leaders. Chang has shown you the bridge from where your concept is today to a game-changing concept that fulfills our definitions of greatness and great financial outcomes. In summary, *find a cultural truth*

---

35 *Eater*: "Ssäm Bar helped popularize Korean preparations like ssäm wraps and tteokbokki rice cakes into America's culinary mainstream [pattern break]."

36 *New York Times*: "Mr. Chang [with Ko] was leading a daring experiment that asked: If you aspired to serve food as original and refined as anything in an expensive uptown restaurant but wanted to keep prices down, [pattern break] exactly how many amenities could you strip out?"

37 *New York Times*: "Bang Bar might make more sense as a provocation than a business concern [pattern break]. It begins serving at 8:30 a.m. and closes when the food is gone, usually by 1 or 2 p.m."

38 *The Infatuation*: "The menu is full of things that should have no business being on your table together [pattern breaks], but you'll walk out thinking it's the only way they should ever be served."

39 *Grub Street*: "David Chang is ready to unveil Fuku [offensive-sounding pattern-breaking name], home of the $8 spicy-fried-chicken sandwich and prototype for what the chef hopes will become a fast-food brand."

40 In a later chapter, I define thought leadership and how to build and leverage it in the restaurant space.

and use it to source an a priori truth that breaks your restaurant out of patterns and on to untread ground that is wide open for you to develop. From there, each step forward will show you additional ways to excite the market.

Note all of Chang's pattern breaks in the footnotes to the paragraphs above. Please don't waste this lesson. The difference between a static concept and an a priori driven one, is that the latter *has no innovation finish line* and, therefore, seeds the greatest possible success in our business. Now, **how you convert loyal customers at substantially more profitable rates** is next. Without the lessons from both of these chapters, restaurants forfeit most of their income potential.

CHAPTER 3

LIFE MOMENT PRINCIPLE

Loyalty is about needs, not points.

IN THIS CHAPTER, WE ANSWER this question:

How do you grow ever-more loyal customers?

Oddly enough, as you will see, this question *bridges the knowledge gap* between achieving:

BUMPY INCOME ⋯⋯→ ACCELERATING INCOME

By the time we had sold our Asia operations, I thought I knew the answer to this chapter question, but then had to figure out how and where to prove it. One thing was clear: It was time to test my research in a venture I had more control over. In Asia, I had to respond to our global public-company headquarters team of great professionals, but at that time we had too many chefs in the kitchen so to speak and this was a watered-down recipe for success that I didn't want to repeat.

With the above in mind, I found myself one hot day walking around on the opposite end of the globe on the fringe of the colonial district of Panama City, Panama.[41] I had loved the city and country for years. Gangs had run the neighborhood for decades and I was daydreaming that I could contribute to its turnaround. Looking for something cold to drink, I walked into a hole-in-the-wall restaurant and struck up a conversation with the waiter-cook-manager who was the only employee on site. He mentioned that the restaurant was for sale. I peppered him with questions and contacted the owners.

The restaurant was losing money and this was exacerbated by what for most would be intolerable realities: the kitchen was smaller than a decent walk-in closet, the dining area had a maximum capacity of 20 guests, there was no dedicated parking, street parking was limited and messy, homeless people often slept outside and pandered for money, and the local gang's drug-trafficking headquarters was literally a 10-year-old child's stone throw away. Every restaurateur who had been approached had rejected the location outright.

For me it was ideal.

Here was a place I could laboratory test globally applicative-concepts under ultra-tough business conditions to prove up what I had I learned. Within 10 days, I bought the business and executed a lease extension with the landlord. I then invited in my friend Alberto (who also understood the hospitality business well) and together we found our third partner, a young, energetic line cook named José[42] who had just returned from Sydney, Australia where he had studied at the Cordon Bleu and had staged in some of the country's top restaurants.

At the time, Panama was on nobody's culinary map because its cuisine was influenced by centuries of immigration from all

---

41 Sorry for the whiplash jump from Asia to Latin America but, since childhood and thanks to my adventurous parents, I am lucky to be comfortable moving fairly seamlessly around our planet.

42 You should follow José Olmedo Carles on Instagram @ajoselegustacocinar. Though young, he is already putting his mark on the world.

over the world, and had never formed a strong identity.[43] The culture was elevated and modernizing, but Panamanian restaurants specialized mostly in comfort food at the time. Back then, there was no standard bearer in Panamanian fine dining let alone for destination fine dining.[44]

To start our development journey, as you now know how to do, we needed to identify a cultural truth that deserved to be broken. With work and debate, we found two cultural truths and one a priori truth that intrigued us:

- The *first cultural truth* was that the market didn't believe that local cuisine could develop enough sophistication to capture international attention.
- The *second cultural truth* was that, because of the country's ethnic diversity, its cuisine had never developed the clear identity of say Japanese or Cajun cuisine; therefore, nobody believed that a culinary narrative could be stitched together to tell the whole story of Panama.
- We used those cultural truths as lenses to define an opposite *a priori truth* that: Yes, Panamanian food *could* be made into a lighter, sophisticated cuisine capable of attracting global attention and *could* tell diners a valuable story of where the country had come from and where it was going.

---

43 Panamanian food per se started when indigenous populations came over from Asia via the frozen Bering Strait and arrived in the region over 5,000 years ago. It took another step when Christopher Columbus made his only mainland stop along Panama's Caribbean coast in the late 1400s. Local food changed again when settlements of Spanish colonists and West African slaves formed and grew over the following three centuries. Many waves of migration came after those original settlers, and they brought culinary influences from as wide-ranging territories as the Caribbean, China, India, France, Scandinavia, Greece and the United States.

44 I define a "fine dining restaurant" as one that offers complex, nuanced cuisine as compared to casual dining, and is seen by *its market* as a sophisticated dining experience. I define a "destination fine dining restaurant" as one that offers complex, nuanced cuisine as compared to local fine dining and offers such a renowned experience that people are willing to travel regionally or even globally to dine there.

Of course, that wasn't the reality yet and that was the point. As discussed in Chapter 2, our a priori truth *gifted* us with the privilege to try to break new ground. It was our job to search for those innovations that would build our new truth into a reality. Me, a non-Panamanian, Alberto a non-cook, and José, a line cook, were going to try and change this little corner of the world.

And here is where the loyal customer question that heads this chapter comes into play.

> **Insight #27: Breaking new ground on its own does *not* make for a durable concept because it does *not* on its own convert NCs or DCs into LCs at high numbers.**

Breaking new ground *does* have tremendous financial value because it excites volumes of new and diminished customers to try you out, but:

> **Insight #28: To build the revenue you need to earn the income you want requires that you solve *identifiable human needs* far better than your competitors do. Solutions to needs are what drive high LC conversions.**

To thrive, we were going to have to solve specific customer needs better than others—we were going to have to become a best *solution provider.* Let's learn what that means.

BUILDING BLOCKS OF ACCELERATING INCOME

Imagine you planted a small tree and your goodhearted neighbors share what they know about watering, fertilizing and, in general, growing a large, healthy one. Years later you become aware that how tall your tree grows depends on how far its roots spread and there wasn't enough soil cover to promote the growth your tree needed. The tree could never reach the heights you hoped for because you and your neighbors were *unaware of what was happening at the root of it all.*

Along our restaurant careers, we are trained and influenced by goodhearted restaurant professionals. We learn everything we can from them on how to grow our business into a larger, healthier one. But there is a problem: Though well intentioned, too many of us pass on mistruths to one another. Please read this insight from David Chang—it tells the story of what most of us face in this business.

> *"So many different opportunities that are missed for people...are because of cultural truths that are wrong."*

Cultural truths or mistruths about how to stack up extraordinary numbers of loyal customers perpetuate *ordinary* restaurant results for most.[45] The reason being is that the truth of how we build loyal customers, just like with the tree metaphor, lies in the invisible underlying roots of why people dine and order out. To bring truth to light, think about the following question:

Do you understand the interplay between customer acquisition costs and accelerating income?

I ask this question because it goes to the heart of how category leaders outpace competitors for even decades. We start with four insights that you *might* know, but likely don't practice:

---

45 As one example, you have likely fallen into the cultural truth trap that a combination of social media, promotions, good food & service together are the best formula for you to build your business. The reality is that these inputs are required just to be in the game. Think about it. Social media is a great communication system, but innovating toward new truths and solving for deep-seated human needs provides the content that enables social media to drive more NCs to our category leaders than it does for everyone else. Without a source for creating pattern-breaking content for even decades, your social media gets lost in the noise. Your peers never understood this, kind-hearted as they are, and have modeled for you an approach that has a very low probability of ever achieving your largest aspirations for the business.

> **Insight #29: Most restaurants generate little to no money on the first visits of NCs and on the first return of long-disappeared DCs. Most also spend far more than they think to acquire an LC and it can take several to many new LC visits to recover that investment.**[46]

There is a measurable cost to acquiring NCs and DCs that you have almost certainly overlooked, but that I will show you in a couple pages (make sure to read all footnotes in this section). Furthermore, to acquire a loyal customer usually costs restaurants 5X to 10X more than to acquire an NC or re-acquire a DC. The next three insights tell you why knowing your different customer acquisition costs is so important:

> **Insight #30: When you sustain the lowest cost of acquiring loyal customers, *you outpace the revenue growth rate of competitors.***[47] **It's automatic.**

That insight tells you that one key to high levels of profitability is how much it costs you to acquire a loyal customer. Now look at this interplay between NCs, DCs and LCs:

> **Insight #31: Two factors drive the cost of LC acquisition: A) The cost of NC-DC acquisition; and B) How well you address your LCs' specific human needs.**

Translation: Lost in the mass of restaurant data is this earth-moving reality:

---

[46] Customer acquisition costs are lower when you are new and novel, but rise overtime unless you can remain novel (see last chapter) and know how to maximize your rate of LC conversions (see this chapter).

[47] Assuming similar levels of marketing spend.

Insight #32: Because NC-DC acquisition costs and solving LC needs are what drive down LC acquisition cost, they are the *most fundamental building blocks of accelerating income.* Impact on them and you change everything.

Let me explain.

- If you can lower your NC and DC acquisition costs, you can drive in more customers with the same marketing spend. Moreover, for each dollar you add to your more efficient marketing, the more NCs and DCs you attract versus those competitors that are not able to lower their NC and DC acquisition costs.
- Since acquisition efficiency makes it easier to attract more NCs and DCs, just by sheer numbers alone you will convert more LCs than otherwise.
- If you are *also* able to increase your LC conversion rate (as you will learn to do in this chapter) from say 10% to 15% or 20%, that means that for every ten NCs or DCs who come in, more of them will become long-term loyal customers with no further acquisition costs.

Efficiently attracting NCs and DCs and efficiently converting LCs are your building blocks of accelerating income because, in cooperation, they are what most stack up LC lifetime values that are the ocean swell of efficient income building. We will now look both at the underlying math *and* at exactly how category leaders maximize LC generation. Their growth approaches might appear on the surface to be similar to your own, but behind their visible actions is a lens that shapes their LC acquisition math in ways that most never observe...at the root.

THE FINANCIAL MODEL OF RESTAURANTS

If you were constructing a 50-story office tower and only laid half of its required foundation, the highrise would always be shaky, right? Most in our business have never understood that a restaurant's financial performance will always be shaky unless it addresses the following foundational inputs:

- Acquisition cost per new or diminished customer.
- Acquisition cost per loyal customer.
- Lifetime value per loyal customer.
- Gross profit per loyal customer.

Acquisition cost of a new or diminished customer: If it were to cost you one versus ten dollars to attract one NC or DC, your ability to finance growth would be 10X more effective. If you lower acquisition costs, you grow faster. Here is how you calculate the acquisition cost of NCs and DCs:

All marketing expense in a month[48] */ the number of new customers and diminished customers that consume with you in the same month*

The formula above says that if you spend $1,000 in a month on marketing and attract 100 new and diminished customers in that month, then your acquisition cost per every new or diminished customer is $10.[49] We will come back to this.

---

[48] Monthly marketing expense is equal to the sum of at minimum the following expenses: Signage lease costs + website maintenance + cost of marketing-related software + third party social media or other service provider + advertising. You could also choose to allocate the cost of team member time working on marketing.

[49] I do not account for loyal customers who repeat because of your marketing spend. The idea is to use marketing to bring in NCs and DCs as that is what will promote the greatest growth through their conversion to LCs. Therefore, we set our metrics only around this outcome.

Acquisition cost of a loyal customer: Knowing how to calculate your LC acquisition cost is a function of your acquisition cost for NCs and DCs. Here is the formula:

Your acquisition cost of a new or diminished customer / Your conversion rate of those visitors to loyal customers

Continuing with the scenario from above, if your acquisition cost is $10 for a new or diminished customer and you steadily convert 10% of them into long-term loyal customers, then $10 / 10% means that it costs you $100 to acquire one loyal customer. That is 10X the acquisition cost of an NC or recovered DC in this scenario. Here is our math so far in table form:

CUSTOMER ACQUISITION COSTS		
MARKETING SPEND IN A MONTH	$	1,000
NC & DC VISITS IN A MONTH		100
ACQUISITION COST OF 1 NC OR DC	$	10
CONVERSION RATE TO LC		10%
ACQUISITION COST OF 1 LC	$	100

Source: Peter LeSar

The above math is within the range of most *mature* restaurants in America.[50] In fact, you will find that the acquisition cost for *most* matured restaurants runs between $50 to $150 per additional loyal customer. You will soon learn how to bring this cost down and to keep trending it lower, but first let's explore the most interesting math of all.

Lifetime value (LTV) of a loyal customer: LTV is something you hear about and yet virtually every non-leader in our industry

---

[50] Newer restaurants in their post-opening upswing years likely spend less, but will march almost quarter-by-quarter to this range. Acquisition costs improve during business cycle upswings and fall during downturns. Don't fool yourself if your customer acquisition costs are improving during an upswing as you might not be impacting on it yourself. By tracking the inputs in the table above, you can proactively lower your acquisition costs with time.

ignores. Doing so is like ignoring a termite trail to your house... the failure to act will someday ruin your foundation. Your market is finite. If one restaurant adds a loyal customer,[51] a second restaurant loses part or all of the LTV of that customer. The losing restaurant also wastes its original LC acquisition cost. Here is how you calculate LTV:

Average ticket size per customer X *average visits per month per loyal customer* X *forecasted lifetime months of a loyal customer*

If your average ticket per customer is $20 and your typical customer comes in once a month and remains a loyal customer for 10 years (120 months), then your revenue LTV from one loyal customer is $2,400. In this scenario thus far, you invested $100 to acquire one loyal customer and that loyal customer produces $2,400 of revenue for you over their life. That is math you can build a business on, but only if you can reproduce it consistently and can scale it, which is what you will learn how to do. Let's go one final step.

Gross profit per loyal customer: Assuming your cost of goods sold are 30% of revenue, your gross profit per new loyal customer from the above is $1,682, translating to a 16.8X gross profit return on your $100 in LC acquisition cost.[52] That is a great return on realistic metrics. Here is how that looks in a table:

---

[51] You should determine your own definition of a "loyal customer". In this scenario, I have determined that an LC is somebody who comes once a month and has an average *per customer* ticket of $20. Regardless of how you define it, the key is that once set, you stay with the same definition in order to measure apples-to-apples progress.

[52] This is not an internal rate of return (IRR) analysis, which would also take into account the passage of time. IRR is interesting, but not necessary as we are only looking for a baseline to measure progress against.

LIFETIME VALUE OF LOYAL CUSTOMERS		
AVERAGE TICKET PER CUSTOMER	$	20
VISITS PER MONTH		1
LIFETIME TERMS (IN MONTHS)		120
REVENUE LTV PER LC	$	2,400
COST OF GOODS SOLD		30%
GROSS PROFIT LTV PER LC	$	1,682
RETURN ON ACQUISITION OF EACH LC		1682%

Source: Peter LeSar

Here is the core takeaway you should have so far:

Insight #33: You don't invest in marketing or improvements to build great results today. You invest to stack up a multitude of loyal customer LTVs that you pay for now to earn income from over many years.

The above is *the* financial model of our business that most restaurant companies don't understand or, if they do, don't build around. The way you build extraordinary levels of income is to build (and keep building) extraordinary numbers of LTV-generating loyal customers. Period.

Between this and the next two chapters, you are going to learn how to optimize this math with simple practices that any restaurant business can undertake. In this chapter, we focus on increasing your LC conversion rates. On the following horizontal page, let's first look at a base case model on the left with a 10% LC conversion rate versus a higher-growth 15% LC conversion rate on the right, assuming all other factors are equal:

BASE CASE RESTAURANT		
10-YEAR RETURN BASED ON *10%* LC CONVERSION RATE (all else being equal and after 1 month of marketing spend)		
MARKETING SPEND IN A MONTH	$	1,000
NCs & DCs GENERATED IN SAME MONTH		100
CONVERSION RATE TO LC		10%
LCs GENERATED IN SAME MONTH		10
AVERAGE TICKET PER CUSTOMER	$	20
VISITS PER MONTH PER AVERAGE LC		1
LIFETIME TERM (IN MONTHS)		120
NC & DC REVENUE GENERATED IN MONTH	$	2,000
LC REVENUE GENERATED OVER THEIR LIFETIME	$	24,000
ADDED REVENUE FROM ONE MONTH MARKETING	$	26,000
COST OF GOODS SOLD		30%
10-YEAR GROSS PROFIT FROM MARKETING SPEND	$	18,226
RETURN ON MARKETING SPEND		1823%

HIGHER GROWTH RESTAURANT		
10-YEAR RETURN BASED ON *15%* LC CONVERSION RATE (all else being equal and after 1 month of marketing spend)		
MARKETING SPEND IN A MONTH	$	1,000
NCs & DCs GENERATED IN SAME MONTH		100
CONVERSION RATE TO LC		15%
LCs GENERATED IN SAME MONTH		15
AVERAGE TICKET PER CUSTOMER	$	20
VISITS PER MONTH PER AVERAGE LC		1
LIFETIME TERM (IN MONTHS)		120
NC & DC REVENUE GENERATED IN MONTH	$	2,000
LC REVENUE GENERATED OVER THEIR LIFETIME	$	36,000
ADDED REVENUE FROM ONE MONTH MARKETING	$	38,000
COST OF GOODS SOLD		30%
10-YEAR GROSS PROFIT FROM MARKETING SPEND	$	26,638
RETURN ON MARKETING SPEND		2664%

Source: Peter LeSar

You should study these tables in detail if you like to deep dive on numbers,[53] but here is the eye-opening story they tell:

- On the left, the base case shows that with a 10% conversion rate of NCs and DCs to LCs and a monthly marketing budget of $1,000, the 10-year gross profit added *from a single month of marketing* should be $18,226.
- On the right, at a 15% LC conversion rate and all else being equal, the 10-year gross profit added from one month of marketing would be $26,638.

Under this comparison, a 5% increase in your LC conversion rate increases both your 10-year go-forward revenue and gross profit *by 46% without increasing marketing spend by even one dollar*. The point:

> **Insight #34: LC conversion rate is an outsized *contributor to a restaurant's financial future*. You must learn the drivers that optimize it.**

Now let's look at the gross profitability of NCs and DCs versus that of LCs.

- In the first table, NCs and DCs generate $2,000 in direct revenue and, with 30% cost of goods sold, only $1,400 in gross profit. If you were to net out 100% of your $1,000 marketing spend here, NCs and DCs would generate an adjusted gross profit of only $400. *NCs and DCs are not a good business on their own.*
- In the same table, LCs generate $24,000 in direct revenue and $16,800 of gross profit. If you were to net out 100% of your $1,000 marketing spend here instead, they would generate an adjusted gross profit of $15,800. *LCs*

[53] Modifying these tables for your store(s) and referring to them in planning meetings can produce powerful insights as to where you are weak in metrics that matter most to revenue & income growth. Again, they are available for free when you text JOIN to +1-813-669-4342.

> *are a fantastic business and the more you convert them cost effectively and at higher rates, the more incredible of a business they become.*

The only caveat is that the vast majority of the gross profit contributed from LCs will come in future years. Conclusion: As stated, you are in the business of investing to acquire LCs now for their long-term income and to keep acquiring them until you no longer have sufficient capacity and thus need to expand.

Let's switch focus to the impact of a 15% conversion rate versus a 10% rate:

- If you hold a 15% LC conversion rate for 12 months of marketing rather than one, the 10-year future gross profit you will have added would be $100,900 higher as compared to a 10% conversion rate.[54]
- If you sustain the 15% LC conversion rate during 10 years of marketing, you would add $1,009,000 in gross profits as compared to the 10% rate. *Conclusion: your LC conversion rate can literally change lives.*[55]

Under all scenarios above, the LC conversion contribution to gross profit assumes zero additional marketing expense as compared to the base case. That is the financial power of LC conversion rate as multiplier of *future* revenues and incomes. When you invest marketing dollars today for performance this week or month not much happens. You are our Base Case Restaurant. You drift with the market current rather than self-determine your growth. On the other hand, when you invest marketing dollars today to build loyal customers who generate demand for you over years, you have more control over your financial destiny

[54] The math: ($26,638 X 12 months) – ($18,228 X 12 months) = $100,944.

[55] The math: ($26,638 X 12 months X 10 years) – ($18,228 X 12 months X 10 years) = $1,009,440.

and can build yourself into our Higher Growth Restaurant that can easily outpace those who don't own this practice.[56]

So, how exactly do you maximize your LC conversion rate?

RESTAURANT CUSTOMERS HIERARCHY OF NEEDS

I love pizza delivery. When the kids want it, I am all in. Ordering pizza solves many needs: "we worked hard today and don't have the energy to cook" or "the kids are hosting sleep overs and we don't want to clean up a messy kitchen" or my college days' reality "I don't have a car to go for food." For me and for most of its customers, Domino's is the epitome of a *solution* provider. They deliver food that is gratifying for most tastes into the hands of hungry people quickly and inexpensively in order to solve many different identifiable "needs".[57]

On the other extreme, when you think about Noma you likely think about the incredible experience it offers: you want to experience new Nordic cuisine or Danish culture or perhaps experience what friends and the media are raving about. Noma's model seemingly responds to "wants," but this is a fallacy because "wants" are not a powerful enough motivator to convince people to spend thousands of dollars and days of their time travelling from around the world to dine there. When Redzepi talks about how far people are willing to travel for good food, he knows that:

> **Insight #35: Restaurants don't serve food as their primary business. They *serve solutions to needs* and food is how their solutions are manifested.**

---

[56] It's feasible to increase LC conversion rates to 20% to 30%, so the estimates above are potentially conservative.

[57] As an aside, marketing pretty much writes itself when you identify a need and provide the best solution. If you struggle with what to say in your marketing, it's because serving *wants* rather than *needs* can make you feel like you are hard selling rather than educating consumers in a way that *excites* their interest.

This insight applies to *every* category leader from Domino's to Noma, and that means it is relevant to your restaurant. This chapter takes you through the need states served by all major segments and offers a range of examples from among our leaders so that you can hone in on the types of needs your restaurant has the opportunity to solve for better. Let's start with this comment by Howard Schultz of Starbucks in the *Financial Times*:

"Customers have different need states."

Schultz knows that humans have a greater diversity of needs than most restaurant professionals realize. In fact, Starbucks serves a wider variety of human needs than perhaps anybody as you will see, and doing so has driven it from humble start-up with a handful of customers to global business with countless millions of them.

As an example of human needs, I wrote this book in part for a "self-actualization" need, meaning that I *need* to be the best person I can be, which for me means learning and growing emotionally and intellectually. I also wrote this book for the very human need of "esteem". I feel a need to have friends and family and you as a restaurant professional see that I have contributed something to the world...that I am worthy of their and your recognition.

I also wrote this book for a more fundamental "safety" need, because I *need* the book to serve others so well that it will generate income for my family. That income helps me to afford healthier food and to be able to live in a low-crime neighborhood, which are both needs around my safety and that of my family. I could have expressed and even believed that I wrote this book because I *wanted* to (which I did, though driven by needs), but that is a superficial analysis of the reality of the human experience for this reason:

Insight #36: Underlying all consumer desires are identifiable needs that provide relative *solidity* around which restaurants can innovate.

If you own a restaurant business or are an executive in one, you likely have the same needs to develop and protect yourself that I have in writing this book. Let's look at the segmentation of human needs as captured by Abraham Maslow, an American psychologist who passed away in 1970. You may already be aware of Maslow who proposed that humans have a *hierarchy of needs*, starting with the need to survive and ending with the highest level need to develop ourselves. As he stated in *Motivation and Personality*, his seminal book on the subject:

> *"...it is reasonable to assume in practically every human being, and certainly in almost every newborn baby, that there is an active will toward health, an impulse towards growth, or towards the actualization."*

As I studied restaurant category leaders, it became clear that customers' decisions as to where to eat fall into Maslow's hierarchy and, in fact, that restaurant segmentation itself is organized to serve different "need states". Below is the *Restaurant Hierarchy of Customer Needs*, in which I merge Maslow's finding with those from my own research. What I will show you in this chapter is that:

> **Insight #37: A restaurant's offerings *must be tailored to solve for the needs of specific customer types* and, when they do, its LC conversion rate rises automatically.**

Review the hierarchy on the following horizontal page and then let's discuss how it impacts on LC conversion.

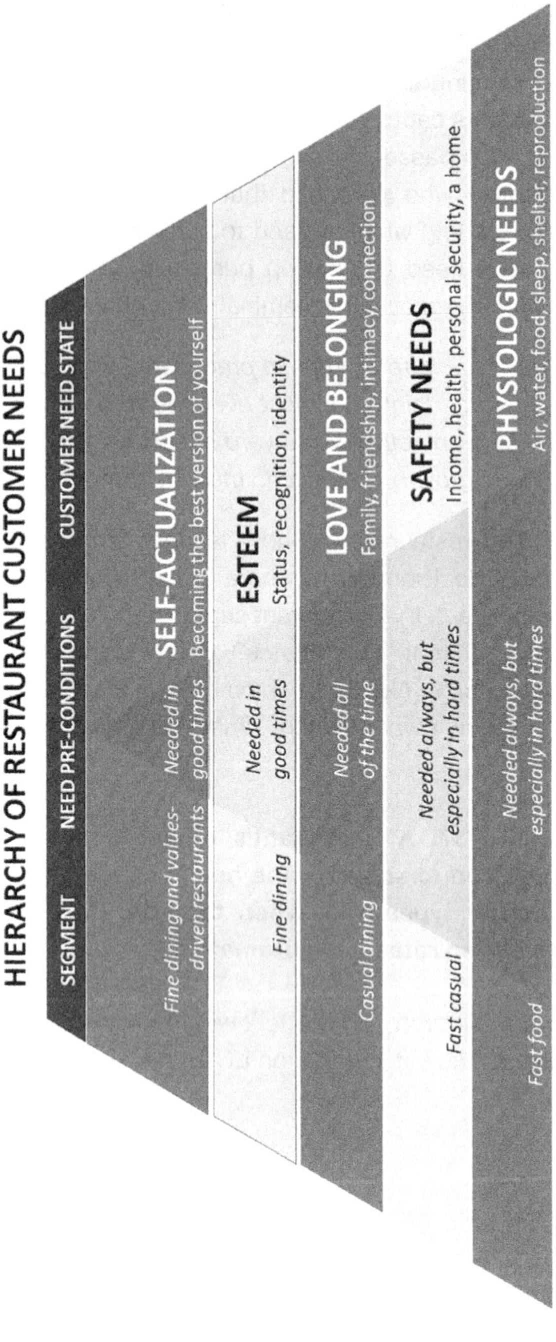

HIERARCHY OF RESTAURANT CUSTOMER NEEDS

SEGMENT	NEED PRE-CONDITIONS	CUSTOMER NEED STATE
Fine dining and values-driven restaurants	*Needed in good times*	**SELF-ACTUALIZATION** Becoming the best version of yourself
Fine dining	*Needed in good times*	**ESTEEM** Status, recognition, identity
Casual dining	*Needed all of the time*	**LOVE AND BELONGING** Family, friendship, intimacy, connection
Fast casual	*Needed always, but especially in hard times*	**SAFETY NEEDS** Income, health, personal security, a home
Fast food	*Needed always, but especially in hard times*	**PHYSIOLOGIC NEEDS** Air, water, food, sleep, shelter, reproduction

Source: Adapted by Peter LeSar from Maslow's Hierarchy of Human Needs

We will use this diagram as a basis for uncovering a number of lessons you need to absorb. The first that I lay the case for below is that category leaders, meaning those that outperform all of their direct competitors, rise to the top based on solving need states as their primary lens for growth. Let's compare three different category leaders to make the point.

Many people love McDonald's or Olive Garden[58] or Eleven Madison Park,[59] and some even love two or all of these very different category leaders. How can that be the case? When you ask restaurant professionals why customers return to their restaurants, responses are almost always *mistakenly* around how wonderful their food and service are. Based on those types of responses, it is easy to conclude that our *primary lens* for growing our business must be on how to improve food and service. Right? Primary lens, no. Critical secondary lens, yes. How you live the distinction will determine your income, so think carefully about these questions:

- What is the rationale that would explain our love for a fast-food giant *and* simultaneously a casual dining chain *and* simultaneously a 50 Best Restaurant?
- Which practices advanced these three restaurants above from humble start-up to category leadership that are *not* practiced by lesser-performing competitors?

When we think of food and service as our primary lens, the answers are just not visible on the surface of how they operate. These questions *are* easy to answer, however, when we think in the context of needs and solutions as you will see. To make the point in a simple way first, when you ask customers what they love about a given restaurant beyond food and service quality, their responses are most often around how the restaurant

---

58 Olive Garden is the United States' leading casual Italian dining chain.

59 Eleven Madison Park, located in NYC, was ranked #1 in 2017 by The World's 50 Best Restaurants.

solves their needs. *I love it because my friends meet up there and they have cute bartenders. My husband and I have our best date night conversations there. It's the best place to watch the game with my buddies.* Restaurants commonly design food and service around the needs they serve (fine wines for a date-night place, shareable wings for a sports bar), but then never fully accept that building best-in-class solutions *must* be our primary lens when we want to move from ordinary to extraordinary outcomes. What must you change when your restaurant business feels adrift? You must identify a set of needs that your company can solve for best as anchors for the future you are building.

Insight #38: Solving customer needs must be your primary lens if you want to outperform others. Product, service and experience are strategically-chosen pieces of your solution.

Restaurants as solution providers explains why a single consumer can love McDonald's, Olive Garden and Eleven Madison Park—each can be the best solution to a customer's needs in certain different moments of their life. It explains why restaurants with delicious food are often outperformed by others with lower-quality food, but higher-quality solutions.[60] Restaurants as solution providers explains why others have outperformed you, but you couldn't figure out why.

Our need states change in any given *moment* based on such factors as the time of day, day of the week, what we are celebrating, if we are worried about money, if we want to connect with friends, if we are trying to lose weight, if we want to take our child's team out for a meal or if we want to go on a date with our spouse and leave the kids at home. We determine where to dine or from whom to order takeout based on these

[60] McDonald's often does not come out on top in taste tests against its competitors, but is the best solution provider in its category and therefore is the category leader.

types of needs and, therefore, you must serve the particular needs of that *life moment* better than others to win our business. Understanding life's moments are your bridge to understanding customer needs:

> **Insight #39: To maximize your LC conversion rate, dig beneath the individual "life moments" of customers to understand how needs vary and then solve those needs better than all of your competitors do.**[61]

With all of the talent in our industry and with the subjective nature of flavor and service, it is impossible to be universally recognized as best for either. Needs on the other hand are rock solid. You inherently understand when one place is better for impressing the in-laws versus another for entertaining the kids versus another for Sunday tea to connect with your girlfriends. So how did McDonald's, Olive Garden and Eleven Madison Park evolve into the leaders of their categories?

> **Insight #40: Category leaders don't always offer the highest quality food or service. They win by solving the specific needs of specific life moments better than everyone else.**

You *can become best* at serving a need and that means you can actually develop a step-by-step plan to beat other restaurants in the battle for loyal customers and for the LTVs that they

---

[61] Life moments will come up at the end of the chapter, but in short describe what people are convening for when they dine with you (i.e., date night versus game night). When you look at customers through their life moments, it helps you to understand their needs in that moment (for example, the needs around "date night" are typically intimacy so we can touch, dimmed lighting so we feel our most beautiful, light food options as we might have sex later, great wine to ease away tension, relative quiet so that we can converse and connect).

offer. How can you make a concrete plan to create the most popular hamburger in your market when taste is so subjective? The answer is you can't and that offers no growth direction. Food and service quality are of course vitally important, but they have to be shaped to cater to the needs you solve best because needs are what give you a clear direction to rise in.

NEED STATES DEEP DIVE

Below are case studies of need states. Note how diverse they are and see how the restaurants solving them push hard into their solutions to drive growth. I suggest you refer back to the hierarchy as you read the below.

Solve self-actualization and esteem needs to become a customer's first choice: What do Noma's customers seek? On the surface, you might say that they *want* to experience new food, learn about Danish culture and experience what everyone is talking about. But if you ask yourself why those wants are important to people, you will see that underneath them lie specific esteem and self-actualization needs as follows:

- *Esteem* is the need to feel respected and valued. Imagine it will soon be your 30-year wedding anniversary. Esteem for your spouse means that you feel a *need* to show her or him that you value the decades of your partnership. In terms of your own self-esteem, Noma might fill a subconscious social currency need. In the telling of your experience, others will be cued that your socio-economic status enables you to take such a trip. Humans are biologically driven to establish our social pecking order, and it is a need that we position for constantly. Virtually all luxury goods play to the esteem need, and Noma as a luxury expense is a *best restaurant solution* to the esteem needs of a 30-year anniversary life moment (or other major milestone) for those who can afford it.

- *Self-actualization* is about expressing and becoming the best version of ourselves. If you vacation in Paris in order to tour its museums or study a foreign language for reasons other than work, these are you fulfilling your very human need to self-actualize. Noma is the maximum expression of sustainable eating. Redzepi and his team work in a scarce environment and have had to make monumental efforts to adapt certain ingredients for consumption to the standards they hold. Those who choose to dine at Noma, when there are millions of other tasty options around the planet that are substantially cheaper, are expressing their need to be their best selves by immersing themselves into the values that Redzepi and his team embody and lead on. Eating at Noma can make you feel more evolved as a person and that is the epitome of self-actualization.

Serving needs makes you the obvious choice when you do it better than others. Solving wants, on the other hand, is too weak for your marketing to translate into much revenue growth. *I feel like eating a hamburger* is a want, but there are often a dozen or more hamburger options in any given market and your marketing to fulfill that want will produce unsatisfactory outcomes unless you also target a need. *I need a filling meal quickly and cheaply* is the physiological need that sells billions of McDonald's hamburgers a year. *I need to feel good about myself while eating a filling meal quickly* merges esteem and physiological needs and sells millions of Shake Shack burgers a year. Excavate for those deep human needs using the Hierarchy of Restaurant Customer Needs, tailor each product and your overall offer to solve those needs better than all competitors do, and then simply market your *solutions* in a pattern-breaking way (to alert people to look). Make this 3-step approach your consistent, improving practice, and voilà, more NCs and DCs will walk in your door, and they will convert to LCs at higher rates than before.

Solve unique combinations of needs to build a new category: As with Noma and Shake Shack, all category leaders solve for unique combinations of needs to sharply differentiate themselves from competitors, while those using food, format and experience as primary lens struggle to build any financially outperforming differentiation at all. Need states, combined with a priori truths and targeted to specific customer types, are how you rise above the market, because:

> **Insight #41: When you serve a combination of needs, it narrows your concept into a unique lens through which you are able to see solutions that competitors can't spot no matter how hard they try.**

SweetGreen recognized the cultural truth that salads cannot be the cornerstone of a scalable fast casual business, and chose to prove the opposite a priori truth that yes it could overcome all of the obstacles (known and unknown) to achieve just that outcome. SweetGreen solves the needs of *income safety* based on their segment, of *health safety* based on the foods they serve, and of *self-actualization* as its customers align to its values of serving ingredients that are cultivated with sustainable practices. That combination of truth and needs (and how they bundled unique solutions around them) differentiated SweetGreen so much that it became hotly pursued by customers, media and capital alike.

When food and service are your primary lens, you shoot in the dark for ways to engage more customers and to convert them at higher levels to loyal ones. When a priori truth and needs combine as your primary lens, you find solutions that are exciting for NCs and DCs and sticky to convert many more LCs and, through both, compound your income.

Solve the overlapping needs of multiple customer types to expand your market: When I dined in Eleven Madison Park, I went with my incredible business partner Salomon Guggenheim and our wives. We were there to celebrate the successful sale of assets after a year marked by challenges. EMP (as they abbreviate it) served both our esteem and love & belonging needs to recognize our work and strengthen our partnership. But there were other customer types there having those same needs solved. I saw older parents with an adult child celebrating a birthday. I saw close friends enjoying their success in the world. They were all dining at EMP for different reasons, but all of those reasons were founded in the needs of both esteem and love & belonging. Here is what you should draw from this:

> **Insight #42: Different customer types can have the same needs *for different reasons* and those needs can be still fulfilled by the same solution. When you can see needs, you can see all of the customers types that your restaurant doesn't yet serve but whose patronage it is primed to win.**

Below is an example of a restaurant whose solution serves many different customer types well, followed by an example of a restaurant that alienated its core customer types by spreading its solution too thinly.

For in-store customers, Starbucks serves many needs:

- *Self-actualization* for customers who align to its progressive values.
- *Esteem* for customers who prefer to be seen there versus at Dunkin' (we will come back to Dunkin' later).
- *Love & belonging* as it's an easy place to meet up with friends and family.
- *Income safety* as most can consume at Starbucks even on tight budgets.
- And, *physiological needs* because you can grab food or coffee quickly when hungry or tired.

Starbucks was *purposefully* designed to serve perhaps the widest range of needs in the industry for the widest swath of customer segments, which include everyone from teenagers who convene at Starbucks after school for the esteem of the brand to small business colleagues who meet up between sales calls and choose Starbucks for budget safety and on to prospective couples on first dates who use the coffee shop to safely explore love & belonging. As Starbucks exemplifies:

> **Insight #43: When your solution solves multiple needs better than others do, your customers will likely find multiple reasons to rely on your business in their lives.**

On the other hand, our second example shows that you must be careful that your solution doesn't attract one core customer type while alienating another at the same time. That example is TGI Friday's. When it first opened in 1965, demand for TGI Friday's soared as its category-pioneering urban singles' bar concept targeted the need of love & belonging for young adults seeking companionship. It was a pure solution provider and hit the cultural wave of women's liberation just perfectly. As it expanded into a chain, however, TGI Friday's took its concept to the suburbs to also serve love & belonging for families in the dining area while continuing to solve the very distinct love & belonging need for singles in their bar. Trying to serve the needs of love & belonging for both was a mistake. The chain alienated both customer types just enough that its suburban outlets were trounced by Applebee's that prioritized the needs of families over singles. The caution: As you point your solution to different target markets, think about whether or not solving their needs might conflict with those of existing core customers.

Here is how what you have seen thus far about needs and solutions can change the trajectory of your business:

Insight #44: As you sharpen your solution(s) and your targeting of customer types whose needs you solve, *you can steadily and proactively increase your revenue growth rate*.

This insight applies for two reasons:

- Consumers are more likely to try out restaurants who *market to their needs* and, therefore, doing so can lower your NC and DC acquisition costs—meaning with the same marketing budget you attract more customers.
- And, when you solve customer needs over wants, customers are more likely to return, meaning you can dramatically increase your LC conversion rate with all of the financial impact that goes with it.

Those who nail needs and solutions can experience a multiplier effect in revenue and income. Here are three more financially valuable ways to serve needs:

Solve the needs served by adjacent segments and take market from them: Casual dining lost business when casual fine emerged and stole away customers by serving love & belonging in a higher-brow atmosphere than casual dining, but at a lower price point and time commitment than fine dining. Casual dining also lost ground as fast casual emerged and used *real* ingredients acceptable to the wellness needs of casual dining customers, but at a lower price point and faster turnaround than casual dining. Fast casual and casual fine both purposefully targeted the *needs* that casual dining served. You too can peel away customers from segments on either side of you by offering solutions, differentiated by your format, to the needs they solve. Even better, it will likely be a pattern break when you do, meaning more NCs and DCs should come to try you out.

Target generational needs to attract a new age group: A question on the minds of many restaurant teams in recent years has been: "How do we attract Millennials (and those younger)?" The short answer is by understanding their needs. Millennials came into adulthood post the 2008 financial crisis with fewer resources and deeper food values than the preceding generations, meaning that Millennials seek a connection between income safety and self-actualization that older generations did not. But Millennials (and Generation Zers) also seek esteem, which means not being disrespected by how they are served. To explain this, think about when you have felt frustrated by the service at a restaurant for whatever reason. You weren't feeling *esteemed* because the restaurant was disrespecting your needs in the moment. Technology and format shifts have led to younger generations expecting more choice and greater convenience in their lives than older generations expect. Ergo, younger generations want to be able to eat what they want, when they want and with as little friction as possible to do so. Restaurants that don't adapt to these changing expectations don't esteem younger generations and don't win their business. On the flip side, those who adapt early can rise with the spending power of younger generations as they move into higher-income adulthood. That could be you.

Solve lower needs on the hierarchy to survive and even thrive in a market-wide crisis: During the pandemic of 2020, takeout friendly restaurants excelled while other segments suffered. Beyond the obvious of quarantines, why is that? Because crises can shift the needs of an entire society in a single moment. The Hierarchy of Restaurant Customer Needs shows those needs that consumers move toward as times harden or improve. In crisis, when we are worried about ourselves and our families, we prefer fast restaurants that best solve our basic physiological and income safety needs. In heady times when the economy is rolling, we move up the hierarchy and refocus on esteem and self-actualization. Noma opened a wine and burger bar named POPL in the pandemic, recognizing that it could generate demand by serving both income safety *and* self-actualization through affiliation with the Noma brand. The result: POPL sold 40,000 hamburgers in its first five weeks of operation. You too can use crises to shift down the hierarchy of needs and do so while still retaining your values as Noma did.[62] You simply need to serve crisis-period needs *better than competitors do* if you wish to rise up during a crisis, rather than fall two steps back (or worse) as most restaurants do.[63, 64, 65]

> **Insight #45: If you adjust and solve for *shifting market-level need states* (be they around customer preferences, generational shifts or because of crises), you can reverse downside risks in tough times and rise faster as the cycle returns to good times.**

If you don't solve specific needs, you won't be able to easily convert loyal customers because people will be confused as to why they need you. If you do offer solutions but they are *weak* as compared to others, it will also greatly suppress your LC conversion rate and your income potential.

Finally, our industry is fluid and improving, and to go farther than others requires that you be faster improving than the rest. *Faster doesn't mean doing more, but rather moving on a straighter path rather than on a winding, guessing one.* Like Noma and Starbucks, your straightest path—and powerful growth multiplier—is to innovate solutions to needs and design food and service to meet those needs so as to both drive

---

62 Most crises are economic.

63 The reason fine dining suffers in crises is because even when the incomes of the wealthy are not negatively impacted (as with the pandemic), they will be more careful about spending in hard times. The point is that *everyone's* needs move closer to our base human needs in *every* crisis, and this is a revenue opportunity.

64 Another note about crises is that they eventually end and, when they do, peoples' needs move back up the hierarchy as they feel comfortable with the stability of the environment and of their income.

65 The shifting hierarchy of needs in good versus hard times is why you see fast food revenues grow in a recession and flatten in periods of more prosperity.

down LC conversion costs and drive up LC conversion rates. Improving that math is what creates true, sustained speed.

I have given you numerous ways to solve customer needs better than your competitors do. Pick a first need and start working on a pattern-breaking solution—the stronger the need and as your solution strengthens, the more both your revenue and income will compound. Your goal should be to build the best solution in your market and to continually strengthen it to hold on to and even extend your lead.

SUI GENERIS YOU

In the Prologue to this book, I described a meal I had decades ago and how years later while reading about "enlightened hospitality" in Danny Meyer's book *Setting the Table*, I reflected that: Hospitality is what makes restaurants great.

This reflection of mine at the time turned out *not* to be a universal truth of category leaders. Why is that? Greatness emerges out of the needs that your restaurant solves better than others, but you have now seen many needs that you can target, not just those served by hospitality. McDonald's is the world's largest restaurant business, but is not renowned for hospitality. Nor are most category leaders, regardless of segment.

Union Square Café, on the other hand, has risen high because its hospitality solves the need of *love & belonging* within New York City's fine dining segment better than its competitors do, which is why it has been ranked first on "Zagat Survey's Most Popular Restaurant list an unprecedented nine times."[xxi] The really important question in this section is: How did Meyer identify the love & belonging need in fine dining when others didn't and how was he able to remain more committed to solving love & belonging than others? To answer that question, let's review a life lesson that Meyer first absorbed as a boy:

> *"In France we usually stayed in low-key family run inns where the welcome felt loving and the gastronomy was exceptional.*

Those trips left a lasting impression. The hug that came with the food made it taste even better! That realization would gradually evolve into my own well-defined business strategy—the core of which is hospitality, or being on the guests' side."[xxii]

Meyer's ability to identify love & belonging as a need within fine dining was inherent to who he was (based on his life experiences) and, therefore, "conceiving Union Square Café as an excellent version of a neighborhood restaurant was, in retrospect, not very challenging." He observed that fine dining restaurants in New York City at the time understood the "technical delivery of a product," but they didn't understand "how the delivery of that product makes its recipient *feel*." Meyer identified with the needs served through hospitality and could self-actualize by incorporating it into American fine dining. This is not about some loose idea of Meyer following his passions, but rather about his self-actualization need to connect the dots of his past to set the course of his future identity. Meyer could never have sustained his commitment to "enlightened hospitality" with a different life experience, because:

> **Insight #46: Your greatest competitive advantage comes from your own need to *self-actualize around your identity* so that you have the staying power to lean in one direction until your restaurant breaks through.**

Each of us is *sui generis*, which is Latin for "one of a kind." Each of us, based on our genes, culture, upbringing, life experiences and our interests that evolve from them, has a unique identity that craves fulfillment.

It takes both intense dedication to a narrow concept and *avoiding distractions long enough* to succeed at high levels in the restaurant business. Most can only push beyond the hard early years of a narrow path when our restaurant concept itself stems from our identities and solves our own needs for self-actualization.

And it goes one level deeper.

Extraordinary restaurant outcomes are only possible when the activities *we pursue as a team* solve valued needs for all stakeholders: owners, employees and customers. On this point, Meyer made a statement that is universal:

> *"...the only way we can consistently earn rave reviews, win repeat business, and develop bonds of loyalty with our guests is to ensure that our own team members feel jazzed about coming to work."*

Why is this true? Because we are dedicated to where we work only when it solves our own individual human needs. The more our restaurants serve not just our basic needs of providing income for food and shelter, but also our self-actualization to express who are, what we have learned, what we believe in and where we can go in our lifetimes, the more intense our dedication—whether we own a restaurant or work in one.

When this 360° needs cycle isn't working, employee churn and owner disinterest both increase. On the contrary, when you link everyone's needs to the mission at hand, your LC conversion rate rises as customers benefit from an engaged team that itself feels more loyal to serving those customers.

> **Insight #47: Those restaurants that experience high levels of churn are not satisfying one or multiple of their employees' needs. Those that have *unusually low levels of churn are solving even the self-actualization needs of their lowest-paid employees*.**

Understanding *sui generis you* as a concept means that you must recognize that all team members are also unique in the world, each with their own *individualized* needs. The Epilogue provides essential guidance in this critical area so I suggest you read through to the end.

OBSTACLES THAT HOLD YOU BACK

Here are two tough obstacles that hold your restaurant business back from extraordinary financial outcomes because you haven't put *need states* at the heart of your loyal customer development practices.

1. *You waste years not building to the level you could*: More restaurateurs than I can count have told me how they "touch every table" to convert visitors into repeat customers. Others will talk about "going the extra mile" along the lines of some of the famous Eleven Madison Park stories of doing the same. These are important, so don't take me wrong, but when literally countless restaurateurs rely on the same loyal customer conversion tactics, you can see there is no real competitive differentiation in those acts and your trajectory will reflect it.
2. *You burn through too many customers*: When you don't have LC conversion tools that outperform those of others, far more NCs and DCs just slip in and out of your doors, and you lose them. When you see an unknown customer leaving and you don't know if you addressed their needs enough for them to return, write down "I just lost $2,400" or whatever amount reflects your estimated lifetime value of an LC. Add up the losses every day and keeping adding them. When that ugly, rising loss of revenue quickly surpasses $50,000 and then $100,000 and is making you sick with anxiety, pick up this book, re-read this chapter and *get your hands dirty* into the work that will change that.[66]

The Life Moment Principle shows you how to move beyond these challenges. Let's get into it.

---

[66] I italicize the words in this sentence in honor of Chef Helena Rizzo, founder of Mani in Sao Paolo, Brazil, who wisely says: "The moment you get your hands dirty, that's when things reveal themselves." [xxxii]

LIFE MOMENT PRINCIPLE

The still-not-fully answered question of this chapter is:

How do you grow ever-more loyal customers?

As you may have surmised, the Life Moment Principle *in part* contends the following:

> *Your restaurant company must solve for one or two specific targeted needs to targeted customer types far better than your direct competitors do in order to grow a larger, ever-more loyal customer base than they have. The more you hone your needs and solutions, the lower your NC and DC customer acquisition costs, the greater your LC conversion rate and the greater your revenue growth rate and resulting income.*

What has not been made clear so far is that there are two easy steps you can take to best serve customer needs.

1. *How we observe our customers matters*: Restaurant category leaders observe their customers using an approach known as ethnography, which is the study of humans in a given environment to better understand why we behave as we do. While I am not suggesting you do the same, well-funded category leaders hire ethnographers to study how customers use their restaurants, so that they can leverage those observations to unfold need states and innovative solutions that convert visitors to loyal customers. An example is Chick-fil-A observing that single parents who arrive with two or more small children can find it chaotic to both navigate the ordering line and to wait near the counter with kids in tow for their food to be ready. Chick-fil-A innovated a solution: Parents could order from the car, a Chick-fil-A staffer

would set up a table once the food was ready, and a parent would just have to walk his or her children into the restaurant and directly to their waiting table. Chick-fil-A solved the needs around the *life moment* that I label "single parent corralling small children into a fast-food restaurant." Chick-fil-A used the same process of customer observation to design their world class drive-thru system. Now let's see how to duplicate this process of observational analysis without hiring anybody.

2. *Your job is to observe life moments and to leverage what you learn*: Let's start with an example. Recently I had breakfast at a local restaurant. In an hour, I observed four distinct groups of women in their twenties who came in to take pictures of themselves with the backdrop of the place, and then stayed to eat. The name I gave to the moment was "20-year-old women, weekend breakfast". The idea is to use a specific name for each moment, so that you can track it over time.[67] The process is to *first* observe what specific customer types engage in and how they engage, *second* to list the needs underlying their behavior and *third* to identify what lessons you can extract to attract more NCs and DCs and to convert them more efficiently to LCs. Study the below and then let's extrapolate the lessons to be learned.

[67] You can label a life moment anyway you want, but I recommend you name it according to the customer segment and moment being lived by the customers under observation. This LME template is included with the supplemental diagrams & charts (text JOIN to +1-813-669-4342).

LIFE MOMENT EXERCISE ("LME")

LIFE MOMENT	CUSTOMER SEGMENT	BEHAVIORS	NEEDS IDENTIFIED FROM HIERARCHY + BEHAVIORS
20-year old women, weekend breakfast	18-22 year-old women in pairs and small groups. Appear to be students from the local college.	*Iconic backdrop* : They took solo and group photos with the backdrop and appeared to post them to social media.	*Esteem* : Published content of themselves that reflected how they wanted to be seen.
		Exploratory experience : The restaurant houses a separate (but open flow) coffee & tea space, small curated bookstore and design-driven gift shop with small luxuries. They browsed all areas. Some purchased and some sneaked glances at young men who were there as well.	*Love & belonging* : Primary connection to one another through exploring items that provoked thinking and conversation. Secondary connection to others who were also gathered there.
		Elevated design : They walked around and pointed to and whispered about design details that inspired them.	*Self-actualization* : Elevated design that, in this case, connected them to heritage details not found elsewhere.

Source: Peter LeSar

Each LME is immediately financially valuable because it helps you to visualize solutions to real-world customer needs. For the case above, let's pretend that your restaurant also has 18-to-22-year-old women college students as occasional customers, and you want to increase the spending from that segment for your own weekend breakfast. Below are specific ways you can drive NC and DC acquisition costs down and LC conversions higher using this single LME:

- *Esteem*: If you add an aspirational selfie spot, it should attract this segment to visit your restaurant a first time. It's a customer acquisition tool that you pay for once, and that works for years.
- *Love & belonging*: Even small foodie or table-top exploratory experiences can offer ways to stimulate connection. The greater the exploratory experience that makes financial sense for the restaurant, the more you should attract this segment. Exploratory experiences fuel word-of-mouth and encourage LC conversions, particularly when the experience evolves over time.

- *Self-actualization*: Even small elevated design details can open up this young segment's minds to new possibilities and help them to imagine better ways of doing and of being. Each time you elevate design in different parts of your business, you should see increased NC and DC visits from this segment as long as you let them know through your messaging. Great design, once paid for, attracts NCs for free and can build and cement long-term relationships with LCs.
- *Overall conclusion*: As you build out any of the above, NCs from this segment will frequent your restaurant more often. As you do all of the above better than competitors, you will likely become the best weekend breakfast solution[68] for this target when most of your competitors will pay little attention to them.

See how easy it is to uncover innovations through fun, creative LME work? Without LMEs, we are blind to easy enhancements that drive revenue, but with them we lead the market in *innovating exactly where it matters*. Here is the impact of using LMEs as a regular practice:

- *The more LMEs you collect for each life moment, the more you can shape your concept around what cements loyalty*: Let's say that you want to become the best in your market at serving women's weekend breakfast. The practice is to find restaurants that serve that life moment well,[69] and then dine at them so that you can build the most comprehensive profile of the behaviors, underlying needs and lessons of the segment living that

---

[68] Assuming of course that you already deliver on food and service.

[69] Proactively seek those restaurants out in your market, in nearby markets and as you travel. Use your LMEs to create a master list of pending improvements for each life moment you are targeting. When you dine out, take an LME sheet with you and take notes.

moment. The LME ties needs, solutions and segment together through research (not guessing) so that you can *best target* that segment for its specific life moment. Other segments living similar life moments also respond to the same solutions you incorporate because their needs overlap with those you identified. Starbucks, for example, has been the most popular place for teenagers in the United States for years. How? By observing after-school life moments and adjusting its products, services and environment to assure that they are always at least a one-yard-stick-better solution than their competitors. You know who else benefits from the sweeter drinks they added to cater to the after-school life moment? Pre-teens coming in with parents on the weekends. Different segment, different moment, same solution...all found through LMEs.

- *The broader your collection of LMEs, the more segments you can build and cement relationships with and, in doing so, the more they will collectively show you how to adjust your overall concept*: Repeat the process above for all of the life moments you spot in your restaurant and you have a business positioning and building system like you have never had. The idea is to dominate the most closely related life moments first so that the needs associated with each can reinforce your solutions for all. But, over time, you can stretch beyond that and you will find solutions that cater to broad need states for diverse customer segments. Look at the history of McDonald's as a case. It started focusing on day workers on short lunch breaks. It observed its customers and step-by-step evolved its solution to serve busy people on the go. Overtime, McDonald's saw children coming in with parents, evaluated those life moment needs, and began to solve them for budget-conscious parents of small children. Today, it serves the needs of people not just at meal times, but also those who just need a quick fuel-up (via McCafé) to make it through the next couple of hours of their day. All of that evolution happened because McDonald's observed the behaviors of the different life moments being lived in their restaurants, studied the underlying needs of those moments, and built innovations to serve those needs.

Insight #48: The more you use LMEs to lead your innovation process, the more effective your conversion of LCs, and the more your revenue and income grow.

Leveraging observation tools to deepen customer loyalty are just one piece of the "greatness" puzzle that category leaders have uncovered. What you are still missing is the knowledge of **how and financially why to fine-tune your concept to lead a category of your own**. It's easier than it sounds and is by far the most effective approach to business building.[70]

[70] A great differentiator between the highest-performing restaurant companies and everyone else is a disciplined, repeatable business building process—*Restaurant Strong* was written to lay out that most proven of processes for you, while DineRock guides its portfolio companies and accelerator clients to maximize financial outcomes.

CHAPTER 4

CATEGORY LEADER PRINCIPLE

There is a navigable path to market leadership.

IN THIS CHAPTER, WE ANSWER the question:

How (and why) do you convince the market to propel you to category leadership?

The answer bridges the *knowledge gap* between being a:

CATEGORY FOLLOWER ⋯⋯→ CATEGORY LEADER

People often tell me that shaping a restaurant concept is what they love most in this business. I get it. It's creative to manifest your ideas into reality and to build something that others love. Concept creation is also about you whittling down to a plan that creates great financial performance, and yet most never nail that target. Why not?

WHAT IS KING IN OUR BUSINESS?

If "content is king" in the publishing business, what is king for restaurants? What drives our greatest outcomes?

Read the following and internalize it literally *forever*. At the time of writing this book, in the United States:

- McDonald's revenue and income are larger than those of its *next 9* direct hamburger chain competitors *combined* (including Burger King).
- Starbuck's revenue and income are larger than those of its *next 9* direct coffee shop chain competitors *combined* (including Dunkin').
- Chick-fil-A's revenue and income are larger than those of its *next 9* direct chicken sandwich competitors *combined* (including KFC).[71]
- All of the following are also larger than their *next 8 or 9* direct competitors *combined*: Chipotle (Mexican fast casual), Taco Bell (Mexican fast food), Subway (sub shop), Panera (bakery café), Buffalo Wild Wing (sports bar), and Olive Garden (Italian casual dining). In fact, the list goes on through virtually every matured category.

In other words, those that lead their category gain a *monumental* financial advantage, often reflected by net incomes that are larger than the next nine of their direct competitors combined. Another way to frame this phenomenon is that:

> **Insight #49: Category leadership is king, because the *majority of the income in our industry goes to category leaders*, while the rest share income crumbs.**[xxiii]

---

[71] Evaluating the US market only here. KFC is huge in China where Chick-fil-A has no operations.

When I realized that *category followers* (meaning those in a category who are not its leader) often share only a minority portion of a category's income, it clarified that you don't want to be a category follower, but rather its leader. Therefore:

> **Insight #50: Your concept must *position* you to lead a category. If it doesn't, your income will be depressed just like that of any other category follower.**

No late starter has ever caught up to McDonald's or to Domino's (in pizza delivery), and the same applies for virtually every other category leader out there. Once you lead a category, it is virtually impossible to knock you down. The lesson: If your concept puts you in a head-to-head battle with another restaurant that already leads your category, don't waste your professional life fighting that battle because your consolation prize for hard effort will inevitably be marginal outcomes rather than those that you have dreamed of. Rather, what you need to do is to make a tiny *positioning shift* to develop a new category, and this is easier than you would think regardless of whether you want to dramatically turn up the potential of an existing restaurant brand or start a new one on an optimized path.

ROADMAP TO CATEGORY LEADERSHIP

Being a category follower makes you vulnerable because it promotes marginal outcomes. You don't want to stay there. You need a road map to becoming a category leader of *a restaurant category that you create*.[72] This is a positioning practice that anyone can undertake once you understand the following:

---

[72] It's possible you are thinking right now that your restaurant defies categorization, and that this is a good thing. If consumers can't create a really sharp framework for why you are relevant in their lives, they can't effectively communicate that on to others. The same applies for the media. You want your restaurant to be "categorized", but just not in the way that our industry has traditionally thought about the subject. This chapter applies to everyone who is striving for greater outcomes regardless of your thoughts *in this moment* about categories.

- What is *positioning*, really?
- What is a *category* in our current age?
- What is the catalyst for a new category?

This chapter shows you how to create a category so that you can position for the financial benefits that come with leadership. To lead a category requires that you learn how to build relationships with consumers on a much larger scale. That is where we will start.

STEP ONE: MINIMIZE CONFUSION & MAXIMIZE RELEVANCY

According to most sources, "positioning" means the:

Practice of creating a unique place for your brand in the minds of target consumers.

How prospective new customers perceive you *before they come in for the first time* determines your ability to win their business. Here is a reiteration of what matters:

Insight #51: The more *sharply defined the needs you serve and the new truth you try to prove up*, the more prospective customers will notice you and come to try you out. The opposite is also true.

To take this a step further, let's assume for a moment that your concept was initially exciting and attracted many new customers, of which a healthy percentage converted to loyal ones. When that early novelty wore down and your rate of new customer arrivals slowed:

How did you excite the market again such that new customer traffic again shifted into high gear?

Most likely you fell back on marketing. And, tried to engage more on social media. Perhaps you investigated some of the shiny ideas out there—AI chatbots, email marketing, influencers and the like. Or, expanded your services and distribution channels. These activities often produce spotty results because they don't re-introduce the level of excitement to try you out that the market felt when you first opened. Once you accept this, you can spot a huge question and opportunity: *If your best ability to attract new customers was at the start of your business, how do you recreate that level of excitement such that time and again many more NCs and DCs are attracted in at your will for even decades to come?*

We start with a basic premise: a radiologist earns more than a family doctor, a structured-product banker earns more than a local commercial banker, and *narrowly focused restaurants earn more than the rest*. They do so because they find both more ways to excite the market and also much stronger solutions to the market's needs. To go deeper, review the insight below that builds on the idea of needs from the last chapter:

Insight #52: Narrowing specialization is how you create growth opportunities.

Narrowing specialization teaches customers how you serve them differently and better than others do. Taco Bell, like with all fast-food brands, solves the need of income safety. It grows by becoming ever more efficient so as to lower its pricing as much as possible compared to other restaurant segments. As technology, infrastructure and consumer habits evolve, Taco Bell seeks out new ways to increase efficiency of production and service, and those ways lead to more revenue. Efficiency as a specialization is an effective growth strategy, but what about after each new round of efficiency has run its course?

When Taco Bell needs to look elsewhere for growth, it innovates to reinforce its income safety solution for *new* life moments. In recent years, Taco Bell added party rooms and party accessories to offer itself as a venue to celebrate birthdays and other special occasions *within its price point*, breaking the cultural truth that fast food restaurants don't have event rooms. Party platform as a service reinforced Taco Bell's solution for income safety *and* expanded the life moments it specializes in, attracting waves of new customers. The point:

> **Insight #53: Each life moment and related needs you solve for as a growth opportunity must reinforce your positioning rather than dilute it. That is how you *minimize confusion* and *maximize relevancy* at the same time.**

This chapter is not about needs and solutions, but about positioning. Reducing confusion and increasing relevancy *fulfill the pre-conditions* required before you can position more narrowly (as I will show you how to do).

Let's start with *confusion*, which caps the revenue of most restaurants every day of the year. Your restaurant missed out on revenue this week and will do so again next week because much of your market is confused as to why they should try you out. The opposite is true here as well:

> **Insight #54: Every time you clear up a confusion, new customers show up.**

Confusion comes in small and large packages.

Typical small confusions include where are you located, what does your building look like, what days and hours are you open, what type of cuisine do you serve and why, do you have a loyalty program and what are the benefits, is your food delivery friendly, who is the owner or manager or chef and what does she or he look like and what is their background, and so on. Allocating just a single social media ad a week to clarify one small confusion at a time will, over time, increase revenue and income. If you make it a steady practice to push that information out to as many targeted audiences as possible within your impact area, you will clear that confusion up for even more people. Want immediate proof? Watch the engagement when you use social media to reduce confusion versus when you use it to sell something. Not only do people tend to engage more, but clarifications make it easier for them to consume with you. It's as simple as: "I don't know what the hours of that place are, so I drive right by it." Versus: "I know they are open on Sunday nights, so let's go there."[73]

You might be thinking "most of my market knows all of the important stuff about my restaurant." And my response is "Your loyal customers do, but probably 90% of the rest do not." Be honest. How many of these details do you know about random retail stores or businesses you drive by? Look at the businesses that you ignore every day and you will see all of the opportunities you have to clear up confusion about your own. Brainstorm on how to let as many people know more about you as possible, put them into action, and new customers will come in.

It's as simple as that.

Now, why is reducing confusion a positioning step for category leadership? Because you cannot shape a category and emerge as its leader if the market is confused about your most basic information.

Large confusions are not about a restaurant's biodata, but about its *relevancy*. Consumers need to understand how you are relevant to them. Subconscious[74] relevancy questions that consumers have about your restaurant include:

---

[73] To optimize these efforts, make sure each of these ads is as simple to understand as possible in a two second glance. It's also okay to recycle ads 2 to 3 times in 90-day rotations (or to let the algorithms run with them under low daily budgets for even months on end). After 90 days, you should uncover other confusions for your next 90-day confusion-reducing campaign so that you break your own pattern.

[74] I say subconscious, because most inputs that influence consumer decisions are received and evaluated below the level of conscious thinking. Inputs provide cues for why we might dismiss a restaurant or try it out. For example, a restaurant with darkened windows might not feel like a safe place to bring my family, so my subconscious mind wouldn't elevate it to the list for my conscious mind to evaluate when planning a family evening out. When you understand how you should maximize your relevancy for your main target markets, you can more easily spot and fix the miscues you present to the market.

- Under what circumstances would I dine with you versus someone else?
- What are you the best at in the market and how so?
- What life moment(s) and related needs of mine do you serve better than anyone else (i.e., date night, game night, family meals, business lunches, quick meetups, happy hour with friends and so on)?
- How will I feel when I am there (cozy, rowdy, warmed up, welcomed, etc.)?
- Why should I spend the energy consciously[75] evaluating you as an option when my habits are already formed around other restaurants?
- What changes have you made recently that make you more relevant to serving my needs and in what ways?

Think about a business you are loyal to. You likely know the answers to the above questions already. That happened through a process of seeing visual cues (signage, façade, marketing) and of hearing word of mouth that cued you into why others relied on that business. The information you received over time made you aware of the business and eventually you decided that it *might* solve a need and was worthy of a visit. During your first visit, you tested the business to learn if it fit for you and then determined whether or not you should return.

Now, if that same business had sped up its distribution of cues and information to *specifically show you their relevance to your life*, you might have started spending money with them years earlier. When you see Applebee's ads showing a parent picking up takeout with a child, they are cuing you in as to one way they are relevant. When you see a Ruth Chris Steakhouse

[75] Conscious evaluation takes energy. Think about when you are in a supermarket figuring out what type of deodorant or cereal or dog food to buy. It can be tiring. Our minds try to avoid expending energy this way, and that is why pattern breaking is so important. We look at the break whether we want to or not. In messages about your relevancy, you must still break patterns to optimize the response.

ad showing a couple on a date, or girlfriends on a girl's night out, they are cuing you into how they might be relevant in your life. There is a juice bar close to my house that I pass by every day. I didn't know they had high-speed internet. I didn't know they served healthy lunches or that they have comfortable places to sit inside. Because they didn't cue me in, I assumed they were like other simple juice bars I knew. They could have won my business through relevancy two years earlier than they did if they had done their job right. Based on my recent spending with them, they probably lost $500 of my business during that time. Multiply that by just 200 prospective new customers that could have seen a fit with effective campaigns around relevancy and that is $100,000 of lost revenue. Relevancy is what turns new customers toward your business, but only if they *know in advance exactly how you are relevant*. Otherwise, prospective customers don't consciously even consider you, don't come in, don't convert to loyal customers and revenue slips from your hands literally every day of the year—including today.

So, after addressing small confusions, you must clearly demonstrate how you are already relevant today. Specifically, I recommend you write down the relevancy questions above and build real answers for them. Once you have answers, let people know regularly through social media and other means how you serve their lives and not just what food and beverage you serve. As prospective customers see your messaging, they will understand *why* they should come in and revenue will grow.

Now, you don't just want to reinforce messaging around how you are relevant, but *actually to build your relevancy*. That is how you grow even more.

Insight #55: Every time you increase relevancy, new customers show up.

A great way to build relevancy is to ask yourself *what purpose your restaurant serves best* and answer without once mentioning your food or beverages. For example, you might answer:

"We serve neighbors coming for community" or "we serve people on the go" or "we serve nostalgia". When you know what purpose you serve best along these lines, you know that as you serve that purpose even better, you will become ever more relevant in peoples' lives compared to those competitors who are static in serving that same purpose.

As an example of how to build relevancy, if you *serve special occasions* as one core purpose, list down the common practices that you and your special occasion competitors share. Let's say that one of those patterns is to offer a selection of at least 30 different wines. A great question to ask is "in what ways does that common practice (in this case of offering 30 different wines) not optimally fulfill our purpose" and then force yourself to list at least two to five meaningful answers. One might be that your staff can't remember the characteristics of each and every wine and has trouble upselling your more expensive wines at the table. A second might be that you don't have the volume purchasing to drive down pricing of more expensive wines. Use those deficiencies to find a pattern break, such as: Let's focus on rarer, more expensive wines as they better serve the esteem needs of a special occasion. Staying with this scenario, you might decide to reduce from 30 to 10 wines, eight of which might be table wines representing the most common varietals and the other two expensive, rarer ones that you buy in volume and that you offer at a 2X mark-up to rotate them quickly. Every month, you could market two new rare wines that you price for people to try out and that your FoH upsells more easily because they have just two products to remember the characteristics of. With better pricing and more volume sales, you could even offer those rare wines by the glass, pairing each to different parts of a meal. You become known as the place that is *more relevant for special occasions* because customers can afford to enjoy and learn about rare wines together, gifting them a topic of conversation to connect over. After breaking that pattern, repeat the above to find other pattern breaks that enhance relevancy.

What you will discover *virtually every single time you do this exercise* is a way to reduce what is less important (i.e., 20 types of wine in your inventory) and enhance what is most important (i.e., access to truly special wines that lift up the celebration of a special occasion). This is critical because:

> **Insight #56: To become more relevant than others requires that you *allocate more resources to fewer things* (translation: you specialize).**

You can choose to be more broadly relevant, but then you will *never be the most relevant at anything* and this leads to poor outcomes. When you allocate more resources to fewer things, however, the market will begin to perceive you have *momentum* as you sharpen your offerings in a relevant direction rather than in a diffused manner as you might do today.

Momentum is just as important as relevance. Let's see a case study for context.

STEP TWO: BUILD MOMENTUM

Did you know Dunkin' has always been as much a coffee business as one that sold donuts?[76] Dunkin' Donuts' founder William Rosenberg said in his autobiography *Time to Make the Donuts*: "Forty percent of my business is coffee" and coffee "was the most profitable item we sold." Dunkin' was the original Starbucks so to speak. Move forward 50 years to the end of Rosenberg's life in 2002 and he still believed the business he founded was unbeatable, writing: "As long as Dunkin' Donuts sticks to the original principles that I established, *it will still conquer*." He then referred quaintly to Starbucks as a "fine example" of a coffee shop that still had a "long way to go to catch us."

[76] As evidence of its coffee focus, the brand name Dunkin' is a reference to *dunking* donuts into coffee. Also, Dunkin's logo has always been a coffee cup on its own or a donut being dunked into a cup of coffee.

Rosenberg appeared to be right in that snapshot in time as Dunkin' by then had expanded to almost 7,000 stores. But we all now know he wasn't. By 2006, Starbucks accelerated past Dunkin' to 12,600 stores and in October of that year announced that it would more than triple its stores to 40,000 to, as cited in a *Boston Globe* affiliate, "keep customers from going to Massachusetts based Dunkin' Donuts." Even more worrisome for Dunkin's future, Starbucks' surge was fueled almost entirely by word of mouth. It didn't need advertising dollars to excite new customers because Starbucks' *positioning strategy* had already created huge excitement around its momentum.[77] Media, prospective customers and even whole communities everywhere were actively watching to see what new thing Starbucks might invent and whether it would come to their area next.

Dunkin' Donuts positioning on the other hand was worn and no longer surprisingly different. It had a loyal following, but it had lost momentum. Why is momentum so important? Because, according to the *Gallup Business Journal*:

> *"It [momentum] represents not just a snapshot of the present but a glimpse into what the future could be."*

Momentum creates market narratives around winners and losers. It tells us who is becoming more exciting and, therefore, who we should try out as a restaurant; and it tells us who is becoming less exciting and who we should diminish our spending with.[78] Momentum consolidates *groupthink* as widening segments of consumers often jump on bandwagons in rapid succession as word spreads. This means you need to ask yourself the following questions:

---

[77] Starbucks launched its first national TV ad campaign only in 2007.

[78] Part of your diminishing customer challenge has to do with consumers' perception of your momentum or lack thereof. Or vice versa, diminishing customers can be the result of a competing restaurant gathering more momentum, and turning your once loyal customers toward it.

- Are your loyal, diminished and prospective new customers jumping on, monitoring the situation, or jumping off your bandwagon these days?
- If they are turning toward a restaurant that currently has more momentum, will they come back because you are more relevant in their lives (meaning they were jumping temporarily at a shiny new thing), or are you less relevant and at risk of falling behind?

Think about your answers. If your momentum is flat or down, you need this chapter desperately. If it is up, do you really know why? Momentum often increases because of a cycle shift and not because we have created the momentum ourselves. Momentum that we don't create is a red flag that when cycles work against us, we will still have a momentum issue.

This leads us to our next insight:

> **Insight #57: A restaurant's momentum is either rising or falling or neutral, and the latter is vulnerable to a fall as well. Category leaders purposefully *position themselves to snowball decades of momentum*, which translates to decades of new customer building. You must learn how this works.**

Dunkin' Donuts messed up and lost its QSR coffee shop leadership. It had relevancy issues and momentum risk. Meanwhile, consumers were band-wagoning into Starbucks and driving high revenue growth rates and accelerating income. Dunkin' Donuts faced the prospect of sharing fewer and fewer income crumbs with a slew of second-tier category followers.

For Dunkin' Donuts, this was an existential crisis. Going head-to-head with Starbucks was a marginal proposition given that market excitement had shifted so disproportionally. It needed to *reposition* to regain momentum and to lead a category again, but the QSR coffee shop category now had another leader. So, what did Dunkin' Donuts do? Hold that thought.

STEP THREE: ESTABLISH YOUR STARTING LINE

By now, you understand that to position your restaurant for category leadership (with all of the earnings power that goes with a leadership position), you first need to:

- Clear up small confusions.
- Clear up large confusions around relevancy.
- Build relevancy to snowball momentum for even decades.

Now that you understand the *pre-conditions* for category development and leadership, how do you build and lead one? The starting point is to make *a tiny shift in your concept to pioneer a new category* as these following brands have:

- Blaze Pizza shifted the typical pizza concept by A) Reducing baking time to 3 minutes; and B) Implementing a build-your-own format to maximize customer choice. Two tiny shifts in *concept* pioneered the pizza fast casual category.
- SweetGreen shifted fast casual by focusing on nutrition over just real ingredients (as Chipotle had pioneered). One tiny shift in *concept* created the salad fast casual category. Leaning into that shift and pursuing the lead of that category elevated SweetGreen into an exciting brand that consumers and the media love to follow.
- Momofuku started as a ramen bar, but its concept was reshaped as Chang searched for relevance and leaned into two tiny shifts: A) Disregard food silos;[79] and B) Disregard the service and ambiance standards typically associated with fine dining. The result: Chang pioneered a pan-ethnic American casual fine dining category that others have since followed.[80]

---

[79] Meaning that he incorporates the culinary roots of all Americans into his cuisine, and not just those of African or European descent.

[80] You might be thinking "is that a category?" The answer is yes as you will see. On another note, ironically, Chang dislikes the idea of categories, but when you follow the path as described in this chapter, a category is what inevitably emerges regardless.

These cases show that tiny shifts do in fact shape new categories and that there is a major upside to doing so. But, why is category development relevant to consumers? They are the ones who jump on and off restaurant bandwagons, so *what is it about early category development that consumers care about?*

The answer lies in neuroscience and, most specifically, in how consumers' brains organize knowledge. Let's begin with this quote from a *Journal of Cognitive Neuroscience* article entitled "How the brain builds on prior knowledge":

> *"It is easier to learn something new if you can link it to something you already know."*

For prospective new customers to understand your restaurant, they must have some *basis* to relate it to other restaurants or perhaps to other areas of their lives. We link a new thing to what we already know in order to develop a juxtaposed framework for that new thing in our minds. This process of framing new or newly shifted concepts makes them recallable.

Steve Ells of Chipotle has frequently said in many forms that: "I started Chipotle with the idea to create an experience that's fast - and not fast food." Chipotle's juxtaposition-structured messaging has guided millions of consumers to understand that if they want fast service *with* real ingredients, Chipotle is relevant for them. Chipotle's position messaging invariably starts by defining what it is *not*, to establish a starting point for how it will build ever-greater relevancy as it innovates its new direction.

Ells speaks this way because he knows that:

> **Insight #58: Juxtaposing a restaurant against competitors *frames* its relevancy to consumers.**

Without attacking any brand specifically, you need to take the same approach. Our brains need frameworks to understand the world around us. Your job is to create a *compare and contrast frame* against competitors and to disseminate that frame so that your market easily understands how you are different and better for them. If you don't, they won't. Luckily, *you are in control of the frame* and get to sharpen it as you understand your relevancy in juxtaposition to others.

Here is where we ease into our discussion on category development. I refer back to this Redzepi quote and then explain:

> *"Scandinavian-Danish cuisine was something quite rustic, mostly known for pastries and smorgasbord cuisine, which in itself has become a joke."*

Redzepi's statement positions in our minds its *cultural truth as starting line* for what Noma is *not* so that all of its progress can be seen as momentum from that point forward.

> **Insight #59: Establishing a starting line allows us to *witness your momentum* each time you innovate further away from the cultural truth you are breaking and toward the a priori truth you are working to prove.**

Cultural truths as starting lines are so powerful that they can position you above the market for the entire life of your restaurant. Alice Waters' Chez Panisse showed Americans the cultural truth that our food distribution system was causing environmental havoc, and became the first restaurant in modern America to re-prove the a priori truth of farm-to-table. Chez Panisse has ascended to the level of cultural icon because we know what it started and how it evolved toward its own version of greatness.[81] The same can be said for McDonald's, Chick-fil-A,

[81] Chez Panisse as an American farm-to-table pioneer owns a broad reputation, but there are plenty of leadership positions one can carve out in any space just by narrowing in. In the Epilogue, I quote Haile Thomas who is a young chef leading a *youth movement* of healthier eating. Dan Barber, owner of the restaurant Blue Hill at Stone Barns, is a leading advocate for crop diversity and his restaurant is a celebration of *diverse, hyper-local produce*. Every broad theme can be narrowed down to find new ways to lead.

Noma, El Bulli in Spain,[82] Starbucks, Central in Peru and Gaggan in Thailand who have all repeatedly *explained to us their view on how the world is imperfect* so that we can bear witness as they reshape it before our eyes. Why else is cultural truth as starting line mission critical? *Drum roll please.* Because:

> **Insight #60: The moment you break a cultural truth is the moment you start a new category—it is also the moment you become a *changemaker*, which is what makes you most relevant of all.**

Categories are *not* made because some higher power in our industry says so. New and powerful restaurant categories emerge *only* once an old cultural truth is knocked out and replaced by a new a priori truth as you now fully understand it.

Noma replaced the outdated Smorgasbord destination category with the New Nordic Cuisine destination fine dining category that addressed ancient customer needs in updated ways and other restaurants saw it work and followed suit.[83] Blaze, SweetGreen and Momofuku pioneered their categories as their tiny shifts in thinking and doing knocked away old truths, which is what your own tiny shift in your restaurant concept must also do. To be clear, no restaurant category was *ever* founded without a cultural truth being broken first. Identifying a strongly-held cultural truth to break is the seed of the most powerfully relevant juxtaposition play in our industry because it shows the market that *you are a changemaker and this is the change you are bringing.*

So why is this relevant to your restaurant specifically?

Because *any restaurant of any size and anywhere on the globe* can snowball relevance and momentum by spotting a culture truth to break, by explaining to us over and over again why

---

82 Now closed, but still one of the most formidable restaurant brands in the history of the world.

83 I will soon define the term “restaurant category”. It will be an eye opener.

it must be broken, and by writing the new category's rules[84] to actually lead it. You just have to focus on it.

You now understand the financial ramifications of being a category leader versus a follower. You also now understand the preliminary steps that can position you for leadership. Now, there is one huge idea left to understand before we dive into the Category Leader Principle itself.

THOUGHT LEADERSHIP AS DRIVING FORCE

As we were conceptualizing our restaurant in Panama, the question we struggled with was: "How can a little restaurant in a small place grab and hold the attention of people all over the world?" For such a small venue as ours to burst through the clamoring for attention of millions of restaurants worldwide would require us to exert a tremendous amount of *force*. The military term "force multiplier" is anything that multiplies the outcomes from a force. It is the term that gave birth to restaurant *growth multipliers*, which I define as:

> **Insight #61: A growth approach that multiplies the financial and impact outcomes produced by your restaurant company while only using the *same force you exert today*.**

When our restaurant achieved coverage in media around the world with no marketing or press relations budget, it was due in part to minimum effort we exerted in one particular area that resulted in outsized excitement.[85] You are about to learn the greatest cost-benefit "marketing" technique in our industry,

---

[84] More on *category rules* in the last section of this chapter.

[85] To give you a sense, we never reached out to any media at all, we never prepared a press release and we certainly never paid money to anyone to help us spread the word, and yet we received coverage from media as wide ranging as *Bloomberg*, *Vogue*, *Conde Nast Traveler*, *Men's Journal*, *Hemisphere Magazine* (magazine of United Airlines), *Architectural Digest*, *The Guardian* (leading UK newspaper), *El Pais* (leading Spanish newspaper), *GQ Magazine*, *ABC News* and *Forbes*.

because it is the one that most richly exposes restaurants to the market and solidifies their drive to category leadership. I say "marketing" in quotes because:

> **Insight #62: The magic of *getting the word out in larger-than-life numbers* has more to do with how you prepare than how you market in the traditional sense.**

Here is a case study that shows you what I mean.

Gaston Passard is the chef proprietor of Paris-based L'Arpège, a restaurant that has held on to three Michelin stars continuously since 1996. That amazing feat is made possible by Passard's *expertise*, which I will differentiate from specialization in a moment. Throughout his career, and as described in the *New York Times*, Passard has been renowned for his "slow-motion method for cooking meat to an unrivaled juiciness in pans that were barely hot enough to melt chocolate."

In 2001, Passard made what appeared to be an insane move. He transformed L'Arpège from a restaurant globally recognized for cooking meat into a vegetarian one.[86] No management consultant would have proposed that choice but Passard knows something about *expertise* that most do not.

Over the following years, he developed himself into a recognized expert on how to use biodynamic farming[87] and cooking techniques to call forth as much flavor as possible from what many chefs consider to be of secondary import—the lowly vegetable. Passard has pushed his expertise on vegetable flavor to such a level that *Bon Appetit Magazine* now calls him "the vegetable whisperer". The result of his decision: Not only did

---

[86] L'Arpège did eventually introduce limited meat.

[87] Like organic farming, biodynamic farming rejects synthetic herbicides, pesticides and fungicides. Unlike organic farming, biodynamic farming places a great emphasis on soil, crop and animal diversity because it operates under the assumption that the three are interdependent on one another in a single living system.

L'Arpège hold on to its three Michelin stars through the entire transition, but in 2018 was awarded by The World's 50 Best Restaurants™ as the 8th best restaurant in the world.

Passard's expertise has attracted more media and customers than a vegetarian restaurant should logically be able to achieve. He is far from alone in leveraging expertise to frame a restaurant's leadership in the eyes of the public.

- The Fat Duck founder Heston Marc Blumenthal[88] built himself into an *expert* on molecular gastronomy, which expertise he has translated into food pairing innovations that lifted his reputation as a leading thinker. His expertise became so established that he earned honorary masters and doctorates from three major universities.
- In our restaurants in Panama, we became *experts* at deconstructing classic comfort recipes into novel, elevated ones that modernized Panamanian cuisine. We also became expert, short-form narrators of Panamanian culinary tales. Combined, this expertise attracted press globally, and lifted us into a leadership position in the eyes of the country.
- Sixty Vines, a wine bar chain, built itself into the premier *expert* on the benefits of serving wine by the keg, which has helped them to make wine more exciting for Millennials than likely any restaurant had done before. The result: Sixty Vines is emerging as a category leader in the wine-led restaurant space.[89]

Expertise takes many forms, and while it informs specialization, expertise must be discussed separately because:

---

[88] The Fat Duck is located in Berkshire, England and was voted the World's Best Restaurant in 2005 by the World's 50 Best.

[89] Sixty Vines offers 60 different wines served from wine kegs, which preserves the temperature and freshness of wines and enables customers to sample from a much wider selection than is normally feasible under traditional formats.

Insight #63: Most restaurants that choose to specialize, do *not* develop deep enough expertise to push innovation beyond where others have gone. Developing your expertise will make you a truer innovator and true innovation is what excites the market as it witnesses you push onto new ground.

Most in our industry stop meaningful learning too early in our careers, believing that all of the learning we need will come through the work itself. The result is that too many of us fail to stretch our expertise into new territory, and that is the opposite approach to how category leaders emerge:

- New York City restaurateur Joe Bastianich became a media celebrity because he worked for 20 years to develop the expertise and gain the experience to make that happen. Now his media expertise attracts customers into seats in his restaurants while his media partnerships compensate him for his personal brand and time.
- Taco Bell *re*shaped its business around Millennials by training itself intensely on the language and expectations of that generation (and on the platforms used by it) far more than others did. Taco Bell's expertise has generated bilions of dollars of revenue.

And to show you how broadly expertise can be put to use in our industry:

- Somali-native Chef Hawa Hassan authored the cookbook *Bibi's Kitchen* that interviews grandmothers from eight African countries bordering the Indian Ocean to showcase the great culinary legacy of that region. She leveraged her expertise to be "seen and heard"[xxiv] as stated in her words, and applied that expertise through her book to expand her reputation to a large media and consumer audience.

Why do I bring up *expertise* separately from *sui generis you* when, like specialization, they seem interrelated? Because:

> **Insight #64: Sui generis you is about linking your identity and needs to what you work on so that you can push through the tough times. Expertise is about building *gravitas*, meaning it's about you being viewed by the public as a serious person who is *worthy of listening to as a leader.***

Hassan specializes in African condiments, which she is committed to because it expresses her sui generis self as a child refugee from Africa to the United States. But it is her expertise to be "seen and heard" that has shown through in *Bibi's Kitchen* and proven to others that she is worthy of following. Gravitas derived from her expertise advanced her reputation more quickly than her specialization and her sui-generis level of commitment were able to do on their own.

Gravitas is also seeded by a second element as alluded to by Tom Colicchio when he acknowledges that as you build your expertise:

"...there's a certain gravity to what you say and what you do."[xxv]

You can't earn gravitas if you don't share your expertise with others. Expertise gifts you *supported points of view* and the authority to be paid attention to, but you must actually speak out to build a platform of followers. Many of us love to speak out via social media platforms, but those that stand above the rest do so based on their recognized expertise. When Colicchio speaks out to garner support for independent restaurants, he shares his expertise *and we listen*. When Passard speaks about growing vegetables for taste, because of the gravitas he has earned through his expertise, we also listen.[90]

---

[90] Gravitas is earned when opinions are swayed by what you say because you have an extraordinarily high level of subject matter knowledge.

Gravitas is not just about what we have to say, but just as importantly how we distribute what we say to best amplify the network effects of our personal and corporate brands. Public speaking, book & article writing, podcasts and earning your way into the media are all podiums that restaurateurs and chefs use to build gravitas and to put *many more customers into seats* at the same time. Expertise used to grow a public platform attracts more NCs and DCs even as you get started, and snowballs them into your restaurant as your ability to communicate, connect and *shape people's thinking* accelerates with time.[91, 92]

Category leaders spin their content as widely as possible through all forms of media. People want to hear what our leaders have to say, but that only applies if what they say is based on expertise and is distributed through platforms that their existing and prospective followers engage with. When you have both earned gravitas and a platform with rising network effects, you are a "thought leader"—an expert people listen to, follow and want to associate with. Don't take this lightly because:

> **Insight #65: Thought leadership can eliminate marketing expense from your P&L and more cost effectively drive revenue than any other form of marketing.**

---

91 There is *no* conflict between promoting a cause that is valuable for your own self-actualization, that contributes to the lives of others and that indirectly fosters demand for your restaurant business. Doing so leads to a virtuous cycle in which the more successful a restaurant business with a cause, the more it has the resources and the gravitas to drive results on behalf of that cause. Restaurateurs and chefs *lead* on many causes including, but not limited to, childhood nutrition, public health, disaster relief, first responder support, social equity and on building resilient, planet-friendly, producer-friendly food systems. There is no limit to what you could focus on as long as it is important to your own sense of identity and your business itself can shape outcomes in the space. Gravitas built through expertise is a powerful tool and if you use it justly, consumers will reward you many times over.

92 Remember that when you change peoples' thinking, we recall you more than restaurants that don't. Recall = revenue. To change peoples' thinking requires expertise, a supported point of view and a platform.

There are many forms of marketing other than thought leadership, but in cost-benefit terms there is nothing close since once you have established yourself, your ongoing cost of leveraging this asset is nil. Once your voice is powerful enough that people want to hear from you, you just use it again for the greater good and customers will show up. Thought leadership is a growth multiplier for restaurants because it:

- Reduces or eliminates marketing expense while raising revenue *at the same time*.
- Places a halo over your restaurant, leading to customers perceiving your food and service to be even better than they would otherwise.[93]
- Makes hiring easier as working for a thought leader is a career-building opportunity, which is also why restaurants run by thought leaders have lower employee churn and turnover costs than you do.
- Makes building a *talented* team easier for the same reason as above, and that translates to higher customer satisfaction and more revenue.
- Increases your pricing flexibility as customers are willing to pay more to dine with those whose personal brand they admire and want to affiliate with.
- Can become a profit center in its own right through paid media, books, public speaking and so on.[94]

The result is game-changing restaurant math. The more you nurture your thought leadership, the better the math. Below is our Higher Growth Restaurant model in which I show financial

[93] Our perceptions of our experiences are influenced by the pre-conditioning of thought leadership.

[94] Many independent category leader founders earn money through these sorts of sideline businesses and, in some cases, earn more through their media empire than through their restaurants.

impact from thought leadership that is similar to those achieved by restaurants that I have supported:

- It applies a 5% higher price point starting in year one, including its pro rata impact on food costs even though price halos from thought leadership can imply a cost-free price increase. This is conservative.
- It reduces marketing expense from 6% of revenue to 4% even though thought leadership has been known to replace virtually all marketing expense. This too is conservative.

I have conservatively incorporated zero impact from better hiring and productivity. I have also not considered that for many of category leaders, thought leadership generates media and sponsorship revenues.

IMPACT OF THOUGHT LEADERSHIP AS GROWTH MULTIPLIER

	HIGHER GROWTH RESTAURANT - LEVERAGING THOUGHT LEADERSHIP						
	Years		1	5	10	15	20
	Food	*70%*	$ 735,000	$ 963,435	$1,351,268	$1,895,223	$2,658,148
Growth Rate	Beverage	*30%*	$ 315,000	$ 412,901	$ 579,115	$ 812,238	$1,139,206
7%	**Total Revenue**		**$1,050,000**	**$1,376,336**	**$1,930,382**	**$2,707,461**	**$3,797,354**
	Food Costs	*32%*	$ 235,200	$ 308,299	$ 432,406	$ 606,471	$ 850,607
	Beverage Costs	*25%*	$ 78,750	$ 103,225	$ 144,779	$ 203,060	$ 284,802
	Totals CoGs		**$ 313,950**	**$ 411,524**	**$ 577,184**	**$ 809,531**	**$1,135,409**
	Gross Profit		**$ 736,050**	**$ 964,811**	**$1,353,198**	**$1,897,930**	**$2,661,945**
	Gross Margin %		*70%*	*70%*	*70%*	*70%*	*70%*
6%	Salaries & Wages	*25%*	$ 262,500	$ 331,400	$ 443,488	$ 593,487	$ 794,220
6%	Employee Benefits	*5%*	$ 52,500	$ 66,280	$ 88,698	$ 118,697	$ 158,844
6%	Direct Operating Expense	*5%*	$ 52,500	$ 66,280	$ 88,698	$ 118,697	$ 158,844
	Administrative Costs & Fees	*3%*	$ 31,500	$ 41,290	$ 57,911	$ 81,224	$ 113,921
	Marketing Expense	*4%*	$ 42,000	$ 55,053	$ 77,215	$ 108,298	$ 151,894
	Energy & Utilities	*4%*	$ 42,000	$ 55,053	$ 77,215	$ 108,298	$ 151,894
6%	General & Administrative	*8%*	$ 84,000	$ 106,048	$ 141,916	$ 189,916	$ 254,150
6%	Occupancy Costs	*6%*	$ 63,000	$ 79,536	$ 106,437	$ 142,437	$ 190,613
	Repairs & Maintenance	*2%*	$ 21,000	$ 27,527	$ 38,608	$ 54,149	$ 75,947
	EBITDA $		**$ 85,050**	**$ 136,343**	**$ 233,011**	**$ 382,725**	**$ 611,618**
	Annual EBITDA Variance		$ 24,050	$ 64,982	$ 146,189	$ 277,093	$ 483,100
	Cumulative EBITDA Variance			$ 217,176	$ 769,760	$1,869,180	**$3,836,198**

Source: Peter LeSar

The net result is an EBITDA increase over our Base Case Restaurant of $3.8 million over twenty years, which is almost $1 million more than our Higher Growth Model on its own. This is a tiny fraction of the financial impact that thought leadership has on the revenue and income of most category leaders.

In our case, we developed the expertise to speak to the Panamanian identity through the food and stories we served. Our unique *point of view* was that the broad fabric of a diverse culture could be stitched together in a single meal supported by narrative. We shared that point of view with our guests and with the media that contacted us and the results were that we:

- Operated with extremely low churn and almost nil labor turnover costs.
- Had the highest-priced restaurant located in virtually the lowest cost commercial real estate—our occupancy costs averaged around 3% of revenue as a result.
- Had enviable price flexibility. We increased prices at one point by over 30% and more people showed up.
- Spent virtually nil on marketing and yet people booked months in advance and paid significant deposits to secure their reservations.
- Often operated at 100% of monthly occupancy, which is almost unheard of (with no marketing spend).

Thought leadership inspires NCs and DCs to really want to dine with you—it makes your restaurant *desirable* which is a status that very few achieve.

If the above is not clear, reach out and let me know what is confusing. Let's now look at the obstacle that holds you back and then learn the Category Leader Principle.

OBSTACLE THAT HOLDS YOU BACK

You are uncertain as to when the market is in control and when you are: An improving economic cycle can trick you into thinking that you have stimulated new demand when you haven't—or vice versa, a quietly weakening market can trick you into questioning your judgement calls, even when they were the right ones. The market drives much of what happens to your business in spans of 12 months to 24 months, *but it is you who is in control of both your shorter and longer-term outcomes*. Short-term, you can launch a pattern-breaking product that can lift your results for months. Long-term, you can implement our growth multipliers and outpace all of your competitors for decades. The market will swing you around between those short-term and long-term horizons. The swings will mess with your emotions, but if you remain hyper aware that your short-term actions will always be additive long term through stacking loyal customers, you can just let the market do what it will do and you will *always* come out the winner over time. Like LC stacking, category building is also a life-long pursuit—look at McDonald's or The French Laundry to understand those horizons. Your everyday positioning work as outlined in this chapter will build your category regardless of how the cycle moves along the way. If you lose sight of the above, you let the market control you. If you own the above and can control your emotions during cycle swings, you own your destiny.

CATEGORY LEADER PRINCIPLE

The Category Leader Principle contends that:

> *There is a singular methodology for developing and leading a category that has consistently worked across time, geography and segment.*

Here is that positioning methodology that *bridges you from follower to leader*, parts of which you previewed above and parts that we lock in now (followed by a case study):

1. *Positioning is a path*: Think about a launch pad and the narrow navigation required to go from lift off to a faraway moon landing. Positioning is *not* supposed to be a one-time set of static food type, service and ambiance decisions you made when you defined your concept, but a narrow flight path that propels you in a targeted direction. Starbucks' third place concept is not static, but a path that Starbucks innovates ahead of its followers to remain the best place to hang out that is neither your home nor your office.[95] If you have a static concept, your ability to excite the market steadily wears off and pulls your revenue growth rate down with it.
2. *An innovation path requires a new starting point* and *a destination*: If you want to explore a new area of forest or new ground for a restaurant, you don't start at an established trailhead as you will then journey on a well-trodden path that has no new ground to offer. If your concept doesn't break a cultural truth, you automatically start at a trailhead that other restaurants have already walked. The only way to correct this is to *now* find your own cultural truth to break as your re-starting point. Chipotle was a burrito concept that realized over time that it could pioneer a new segment that incorporated real ingredients into fast food. Course correcting mid-journey is the norm. From whatever new truth you uncover, you must then travel toward a targeted position so you are not spinning in place. All journeys that excite markets (with a priori truth) and sustain the interest of customers long term (with solutions to needs) must navigate toward an almost seemingly impossible

[95] In Starbucks' early days, few believed Schultz that Americans needed a third place. Breaking a cultural truth usually seems crazy and will be criticized *until it is broken by someone*—at which point people tend to see it as obvious and wonder why they missed it. Many of us feel uncomfortable breaking from existing norms and lose opportunities to break from them. Don't let that be you.

destination—a one-of-a-kind *customer-facing end goal* that incorporate both characteristics.

3. *Innovations are found through customer-facing end goals framed as questions*: Starbucks' as third place is a starting point, a path and a moon shot of a customer-facing end goal all wrapped in one. How so? Since Schultz took over the brand in 1987, Starbucks never stopped asking itself this question: *how can Starbucks be an even better place to hang out tomorrow than today?* It has pointed this question for years at every single aspect of its business, guard railing its innovations along a single, narrow flight path. Without that question, we would probably not know about Starbucks at all. *The question means everything*. You need a similarly structured question (leaving the underlined words of Starbucks' question intact) that you ask yourself every day vis-à-vis your restaurant. The question must consolidate both your a priori truth and the core need you solve for, just as Starbucks' question does. Once you figure the question out and then relentlessly pursue its answer, you will find the innovations you need to advance beyond competitors who never take this approach. The customer-facing end goal as a question is a growth multiplier because it focuses you every day on what counts for the long term. Most restaurants drift in search of a value proposition, but the customer-facing end goal as a question structures that value proposition for you. It gifts you what you have been looking for—a straight, faster path forward. As with Starbucks, the sharper your question, the more consumer confusion will wash away, relevancy will sharpen and, with each new innovation, the more the market will see your momentum and turn toward you as a category leader rewarding you with the financial benefits that go with that status. To maximize the growth multiplier effect, you need to find the right question using the structure above, point it at all aspects of your business,

and answer it with innovations that take you to that end goal where no one else will ever journey without having the same exact question.

4. *It's the rules, follower*: In 1992, political advisor James Carville coined the expression "It's the economy, stupid." Since then, regardless of one's political affiliations, we have all understood that people usually vote based on their own fears or dreams about their financial future. "It's the *rules*, follower" is my attempt to help you to see the following with clarity: *as you innovate your category forward you simultaneously write the rules for it.* Look closely at Starbucks' innovations in this footnote[96] and you will see that their practices became the institutionalized rules for the way modern coffee shops operate. If you want to open up a QSR coffee shop today, consumers will expect you to comply with their understanding of

[96] Here are just a few of the rules that Starbucks wrote that shaped its category and that are now followed by virtually all coffee shops: A) Starbucks imposes no service protocols as compared to sit down restaurants, which usually require minimum orders, expect that you purchase a full meal, require that you signal servers when you need service and expect large tips; B) Starbucks offers you a place in which you can come in for a 5-minute meeting with someone or stay and work for hours, meaning there is total flexibility as to how you use their facility as compared to most restaurants; C) So that people can work more effectively, Starbucks was the first chain to offer free, high-speed Wi-Fi, outlets at every table, tables sized for 2 or 4 laptops, and community tables for larger working groups; D) So that customers can hang out during any mealtime, Starbucks developed sandwiches that work for breakfast, lunch and dinner and added accessory snacks that you can purchase to build your own full meal; E) So that people are comfortable hanging out between meals, Starbucks populated it's menu and grab n' go area with snack items that are attractive anytime of the day; F) Starbucks developed colorful, sweeter coffee-based drinks so that teens feel excited to hang out there after school (which also attract preteens); and G) Because you want a hangout place that esteems you, Starbucks employees are trained to ask your name and call it out when your items are ready. These innovations are now the new cultural truths that trap most coffee shops in Starbucks' wake, while Starbucks keeps looking for its next pattern breaking move to push the category forward.

Dunkin' *changed its customer-facing end goal and that changed its category*, gifting it with renewed relevance, momentum and an opportunity to lead again.

Before diving deep on Dunkin', it's important to grasp the impact of *differentiation over time*. Tiny navigational shifts in space travel move you off course by even millions of miles—the longer and farther you travel, the *more differentiated* your path becomes from all other space ships. The same applies for restaurants:

A tiny concept shift continually innovated into over its long, narrow path, forever increases a restaurant's differentiation away from everyone else.

That is the core business strategy of category leaders—to innovate narrowly over years and decades so that they become *ever-more* differentiated. A static concept can never differentiate enough to hold a lead for long. A restaurant navigating along its own long, narrow path is almost impossible to catch up to because by the time you do, it will have already innovated three more steps forward.

As you will see, in resetting its customer-facing end goal, Dunkin' gifted itself a new destination to innovate toward that was unfettered by direct competition with Starbucks' third-place path. Once on its own path, Dunkin' then innovated forward to regain its relevance, momentum and leadership. It didn't need a master plan up front, but just a path bookended and guard railed by a cultural truth as starting line and customer-facing end goal as destination.

In order for us to properly look at the concept shift made by Dunkin', we must first formally update the definition of "restaurant category". The current definition suppresses restaurant revenue and income when relied on. It's time to change that. We start with the term "category" on its own, which Oxford Dictionaries defines as:

> "1) A class or division of people or things regarded as having particular *shared characteristics*. 2) One of a

possibly *exhaustive set of classes* among which all things might be distributed. 3) One of the *a priori* conceptions applied by the *mind* to sense impressions."

Ergo, a "restaurant category" can be anything among an *exhaustive set of classes*, must have some *shared characteristics* with others, and is determined by how human *minds* organize information based on perceptions of the world.

In other words, categories are not top-down designations made by some obscure restaurant industry leaders, but are bottom-up determinations made based on how consumers' minds converge in groupthink on ways to organize our shared world. Here is what few in our business understand: *you as a restaurateur can create the frame that shapes how groupthink evolves, including in your favor.*

Yes, our industry can pound the idea that fast food hamburgers *a la* McDonald's is a category and consumers will believe it. Or that fast casual burgers are a different category a la Shake Shack. But you can hammer back the idea that Japanese fast fine pork belly burgers (for example) is its own category *as long as you innovate real rules to the category that consumers can frame in their minds* and that others in seeing your success deem worthy of copying.

New Nordic destination fine dining was *not* a category until Noma gave it physical definition and consumers bought into it as a result. Pan-ethnic American casual fine was *not* a category until the Momofuku group of restaurants gave definition to it and consumers understood it. Neither Redzepi nor Chang might label what they have accomplished as a new category, but semantics aside, it is what they have achieved. *Category leaders start as categories of one* and then others eventually follow. How sharp the definition of your adjusted concept is and how often and loudly you share that definition are the keys to assuring your market frames your concept as a new category of which you are its early leader.

Let's return to Dunkin' and see how this works. In April 2006, Dunkin' publicly announced the following moves:

- Changed its tagline to "America runs on Dunkin'", signaling that it was adopting a new customer-facing end goal as you will see.[99]
- In conjunction with that tagline, announced that it was undertaking the "most significant *repositioning* effort in the company's 55-year history" that "focuses on American values of hard work and fun."
- Its stated intent was to "revolutionize the brand's *position* by focusing on how Dunkin' Donuts keeps *busy Americans fueled and on the go*."

Dunkin's new customer-facing end goal? For it to become the best place to serve *busy Americans* who didn't have time to hang out in a third place, but who just wanted to fuel up and go. In doing so, Dunkin' broke two cultural truths of the time and replaced them with two a priori truths of its own:

- *Cultural truth 1*: That coffee shops must *feel* like aspirational, lifestyle choices which is the truth that Starbucks brought to its shops and that most coffee shops accepted as a rule of the category. *A priori truth 1*: Dunkin's coffee shops are for everyday Americans who *value hard work and fun* (i.e., sugary, colorful donuts are more fun than Starbucks' offerings) over what it implies are leisurely, elitist values of hanging out.[100]
- *Cultural truth 2*: That coffee shops must solve the need states that a hanging out place does, which creates added real estate and table turn costs that are built into Starbucks' higher pricing. *A priori truth 2*: That coffee

---

[99] Tagline changes by chains always signal that their growth was running out of steam and that they had uncovered an adjusted customer-facing end goal that would likely renew their growth.

[100] Dunkin's "American" truth is in direct juxtaposition to Starbucks' own "3rd place" a priori truth founded on the European ideal of the Italian expresso bar. Dunkin' has framed that it is designed to serve middle class Americans by creating a juxtaposed frame that Starbucks is elitest.

shops can choose to solve the need states of fast food, meaning they can innovate more convenient locations, lower pricing, speedier turns and a greater focus on comfort food than did Starbucks at the time.

How did Dunkin' innovate into its new direction to prove up its new truths?

- With its franchisees, it began to build outlets in gas stations, hyper markets and airports that brought Dunkin' to busy American *on-the-go* foot traffic rather than pushing customers to travel to higher-brow locations.
- It expanded the grab n' go area in their stores so that people could move quickly through them.
- It undercut Starbucks in pricing across the board to solve the central fast food need of income safety.
- It added more drinks that are sweet and/or that *fuel Americans* in *fun* ways (i.e., Dunkin' Energy Punch) and it added more comfort food (i.e., donut fries), *repositioning* against the cultural truth of the time that coffee shop food should feel elevated and unprocessed.

Chief Marketing Officer Tony Weisman clarified in an interview on *Beet.TV* in 2019 that Dunkin' had to change its course trajectory in order to change its future:

> *"If we keep serving the same product to the same consumers in the same way, over time we're going to go the way of a lot of other retail brands in recent years."*

He then framed the new direction by using *juxtaposition* to show that it was the *opposite* of a culturally elite hangout space:

> *"Everything we do is about speed. There are plenty of places you can go to write the next great American novel. Not Dunkin'."*

With this statement, Weisman did his job as you need to do yours. He *re-categorized* the relevance Dunkin' would have in our lives. He leveraged the reality that categories are what we can frame bottom up in consumers' minds. Dunkin's repositioning gifted it an opportunity to lead again with its own a priori truths and its own solutions to the identifiable needs of a targeted set of customer types.

The result: Dunkin's revenues grew from around $500 million in 2007 to just under $1.4 billion in 2019. This is a revenue increase of around 165% or approximately *double the revenue growth rate* for the U.S. restaurant market as a whole even though Dunkin' was already a 60-year-old brand at the time.

Dunkin's outcome is reflective of what is possible for any restaurant business when it needs to ignite growth again. You too can take advantage of these approaches, if you just take the first few steps and then stay the course. It's now time for our last chapter in which all you have learned is laid out **in a step-by-step process of growth and development.**

CHAPTER 5

GROWTH MODEL PRINCIPLE

The step-by-step Growth Model of category leaders starting with how they define a "restaurant concept".

IN THIS FINAL CHAPTER, I answer the following:

How do you bring everything you have learned together into a straight-forward process of growth and development?

Before we dive in, allow me to state gently that in relation to *out*performance, you, your colleagues and your restaurant company likely all operate in a permanent state of *cognitive dissonance*, which is defined by Oxford Dictionaries as:

"inconsistent thoughts, beliefs, or attitudes, especially as relating to behavioral decisions and attitude change."

Every senior member of my team in Asia (including me) suffered from cognitive dissonance around issues of restaurant growth and outperformance. We had trouble deciding with confidence on which menu change ups would attract the most customers, which promotions would build our market share, how to permanently raise our visibility above that of our aggressive competition and so on. This is your challenge as well and, without you seeing it at the time, your cognitive dissonance began the *moment you defined your restaurant's concept.*[101]

Here is an analogy for clarity. When you want as much certainty as possible that you can build a great meal, you first design a recipe for greatness and then you buy the ingredients. You don't first choose a few random ingredients and then try to invent a recipe around them. The meal might come out surprisingly well in this manner, but its *probability* of achieving greatness is far, far lower.

Likewise, when we first choose the ingredients (food, format, ambiance) for a concept, and second try to build a recipe for success around them, our probability of outperforming competitors long term falls dramatically. Graphically, the *underperforming* versus *outperforming* methodologies for building a restaurant concept are as follows:

How concepts that *underperform* (and create cognitive dissonance around growth) are designed			How concepts that *outperform* (and create cognitive consistency around growth) are designed		
INGREDIENTS		**GROWTH RECIPE**	**GROWTH RECIPE**		**INGREDIENTS**
Food	〉	Culture	Culture	〉	Food
Format		Needs	Needs		Format
Ambiance		Positioning	Positioning		Ambiance

Source: Peter LeSar

101 Interestingly, customers frequently experience cognitive dissonance when they feel a conflict *between two or more needs*. Conflicts between competing needs present opportunities to build new solutions, like these you have already seen: A salad served with a protein added on top (i.e., grilled chicken or salmon) solves our need to eat light *and* our physiological need to feel satiated. Non-alcoholic beer solves our love & belonging need by supporting us hanging out in a bar *and* our safety need of not drinking and driving. Gluten-free anything solves well-being needs *and* physiological needs to consume carbs. High-top tables solve our love & belonging need to hang out with like-minded bar patrons and our love & belonging need to sit more intimately with multiple family members or friends than a bar counter permits.

When you start with your physical outputs of food, format and ambiance, it is hard to associate them in a cognitively consistent way to the category leader's recipe for growth. Here are two of countless examples of concepts that usually start the wrong way and hit hard growth ceilings as a result:

- *Barbeque restaurants* commonly hit growth ceilings because they are defined rigidly by a cooking technique and perhaps by a particular style of barbeque. Concepts based on cooking technique often stall because they can't find ways to connect to customers that are sufficiently differentiated from what their competitors do.
- *Thai restaurants* or any restaurant paying strict adherence to the norms of a cuisine also commonly hit growth ceilings because they see no way to build a relationship with customers that is materially distinct from how other similarly conceived restaurants operate.[102]

In both cases and for the vast majority of restaurants operating today, their pattern breaking is limited by their tactical understanding of what a restaurant concept is supposed to be. Restaurants like these might continue to operate for many years, but rarely as financially exciting businesses because their ability to extend their differentiation from competitors hits a wall. On the reverse side, when a restaurant outpaces its competition for many years, it is because its concept is structured to promote ever-growing differentiation. The *Category Leaders' Concept Architecture* will guide you on how to do the same.

[102] I love Thai food and use it only as an example. The same can be said for any other cuisine that has a set of norms to it that are not filtered through a unique, properly structured point of view.

CATEGORY LEADERS' CONCEPT ARCHITECTURE

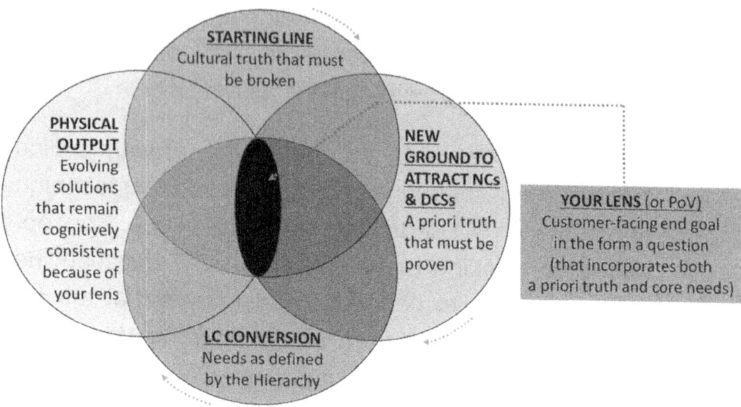

Source: Peter LeSar

If you want to develop a concept that can sustain high rates of revenue growth,[103] the above shows you how (and translates everything you have learned into a single process):

1. Start at the starting line at the top by finding a cultural truth to break—when beginning this step, re-read Chapter 2 to remember how this works.
2. Move clockwise and use your cultural truth to spot an a priori truth—again, re-read Chapter 2.
3. Continuing clockwise, use the Hierarchy of Restaurant Customer Needs and Life Moment Exercises to uncover the best human needs for your restaurant to solve—re-study Chapter 3 to do this correctly.
4. Use the inputs above to identify your own unique solutions to customer needs and customer targets. Again, review Chapter 3 to do this the right way.

---

[103] This concept architecture is included with the other supporting materials at the web site.

5. Develop your customer-facing end goal of a question to uncover (as taught in Chapter 4) and then launch pattern-breaking (to attract NCs and DCs), needs-solving (to convert LCs) innovations—this Chapter 5 deep dives on both how to innovate and how to launch.
6. When growth slows, use your question to find and launch your next pattern-breaking innovation. Repeat forever to attract wave-after-wave of NCs and DCs, converting them to LCs at higher rates as you do.
7. Years from now, once customers have taken up your a priori truth as a new cultural truth,[104] rethink where your company might lead next. If your question no longer shows you the way, update it and try again—study how Dunkin' did this at the end of Chapter 4, but also see the coming Taco Bell case study.

Now, see how Noma applied this architecture:

[104] All a priori truths that win the war of ideas eventually become cultural truths themselves, now vulnerable to a new generation of a priori truth seeking innovators. Bringing systems of production and logistics into restaurants used to be an a priori truth, but was taken up by fast food and is now a cultural truth. Farm to table was an a priori truth, but now is a cultural truth. That "American" food should reflect the roots of all American citizens (and not just those of European and African descent) is still an a priori truth, but steadily gaining acceptance and will likely someday be yet another cultural truth ready for the next generation to knock down. A priori truths knocking down cultural truths and then, through increasing acceptance, evolving into cultural truths themselves is the beating heart of how our industry innovates forward.

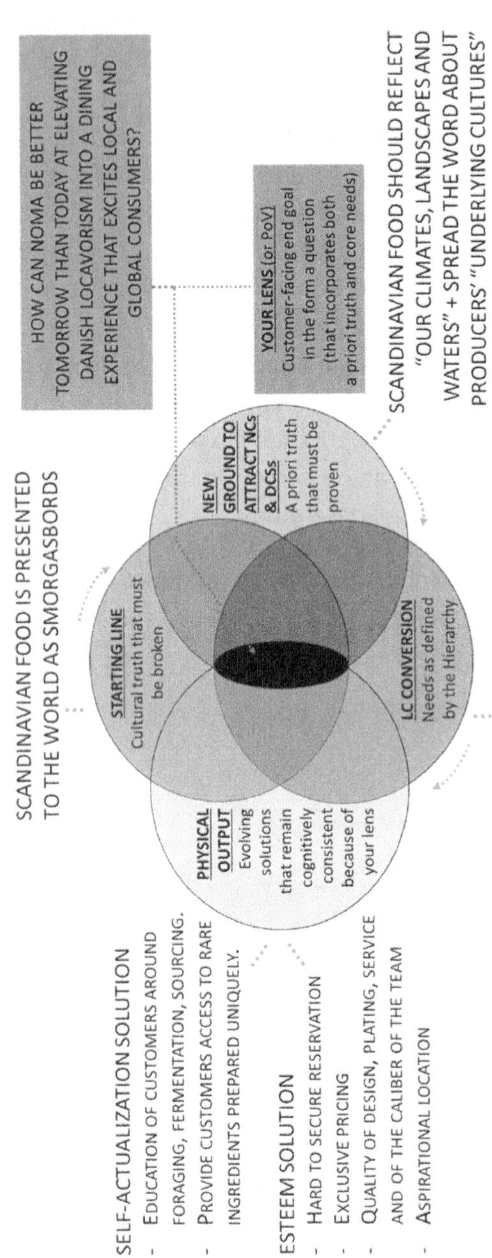

Source: Peter LeSar

As the five-time winner of the World's Best Restaurant, Noma fully leveraged this architecture as follows:

- They looked through the lens of their *customer-facing end goal in the form of a question* (see upper right box) to shape all major decisions. That question is derived from the meeting point of our core growth multipliers (cultural truth, a priori truth, needs and solutions).
- The lens as a question inquires how Noma will be better at serving its customer-facing end goal *tomorrow versus today*. This question (with this exact structure) forces you to treat your concept as fluid and not as static. Ask your question to yourself and team in every meeting.
- Because the question guided Noma away from its original cultural truth (smorgasbords) and toward its a priori truth (that Nordic cuisine should rely on ingredients found in its "climates, landscapes and waters"), it innovated them away from competitors and toward their own category to lead on. The same should happen for your restaurant business if you use this process.[105]

[105] If you are a community-focused restaurant, you still need this method. As an example, let's assume for the moment that in your community there is a cultural truth that political, ethnic and/or generational division is too strong to convince a diversity of people to support one another. In this case, your potential customer-facing end goal of a question might be: *"How can I get better tomorrow than today at helping people of all backgrounds to connect and understand that we all share common aspirations?"* How do you innovate into that question? You could use closed hours for community meetings. You could host three-generation days in which three-generation tables get 10% off their tab. You could do the same with multi-ethnic table days, which would certainly create a lot of buzz and controversy and dialogue. You could organize Policy Mondays where public policies are discussed on the first Monday of each month, supported by local speakers. You could celebrate all aspects of your community and show why they are worthy of celebrating. The opportunities to put yourself at the center of community are endless, powerful and profitable if you lean into the question.

Here is how using this concept architecture helped Noma to build a concept that became globally renowned:

The more Noma said "yes" to actions and behaviors that were cognitively consistent with its lens and "no" to those that were not, the narrower and more powerfully unique its value proposition became in the market's eyes.

Noma's adherence to its narrow question intensified its value so powerfully that consumers from all over the world have reorganized vacations, tightened budgets and jumped through pain points to travel to Noma. If Noma had decided to incorporate imported ingredients into its cuisine after a few years, the intensity of its value would be less than it is today. The *duration* of your commitment to your customer-facing end goal of a question is critical, because it is the compounding of narrowed innovations over time that transform ordinary value propositions into financially powerful, expansive ones.

Insight #66: The boundaries of what to do and what not to do, combined with having an end goal of where you need to go on behalf of customers, collectively guardrail a restaurant forward rather than making them feel adrift as those that rely on the traditional definition of concept experience.

Noma's narrow lens is also unusually flexible. Because it is not trapped by outdated cultural truths:

Noma can introduce almost any product, service, experience or other type of solution it wants as long as it is cognitively consistent with its lens. That means it can flexibly adjust to challenges and trend changes far more smoothly and completely than a fine dining restaurant with a static concept.

Flexibility in a concept promotes resilience. Resilience compounds higher incomes for more years. Humans overestimate the short-term impact of what we dedicate our time to (i.e., you overestimated how much you would make from your business short-term), but we *way underestimate* the long-term income that can accrue from a resilient concept. Taking into account the above, below is an optimized definition of "restaurant concept". The architecture is a visual of this definition.

> A *restaurant concept* is not static, but a path that: A) Is differentiated by how you juxtapose against everyone else (breaking cultural truth); B) Is narrowed by your unique set of beliefs (a priori truth) and by the customer needs you serve (hierarchy of needs); C) Is flexible enough that you can resiliently adjust your solutions to an evolving marketplace; and D) Pushes you to innovate answers to your customer-facing end goal of a question so that you can develop and lead a category of your own.

WHAT IS MCDONALD'S CONCEPT, REALLY?

For further proof that this definition is the one that category leaders rely on, ask yourself how McDonald's as a hamburger QSR could have possibly branched out to chicken sandwiches, nuggets, fish sandwiches, salads and coffee. If we believed that food type, service format and ambiance were the foundations of concept (rather than the output of your growth recipe), we would have to ask whether or not McDonald's is a hamburger joint, a sandwich place, a coffee place or even something else. But because McDonald's real concept has never been a hamburger QSR, but rather as described on the opposite page, it has *even moved entirely away from hamburgers* when conditions required it to. I will prove this statement to you in a minute.

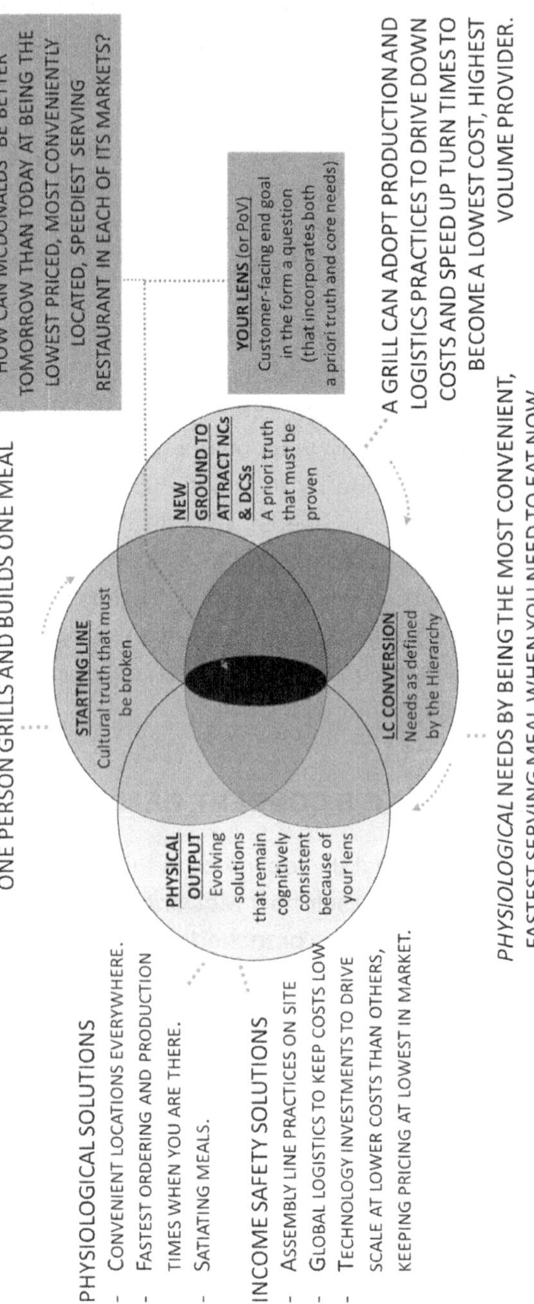

ARCHITECTURE OF MCDONALD'S CONCEPT
ONE PERSON GRILLS AND BUILDS ONE MEAL
HOW CAN MCDONALDS' BE BETTER TOMORROW THAN TODAY AT BEING THE LOWEST PRICED, MOST CONVENIENTLY LOCATED, SPEEDIEST SERVING RESTAURANT IN EACH OF ITS MARKETS?
YOUR LENS (or PoV)
Customer-facing end goal in the form a question (that incorporates both a priori truth and core needs)
STARTING LINE
Cultural truth that must be broken
NEW GROUND TO ATTRACT NCs & DCSs
A priori truth that must be proven
LC CONVERSION
Needs as defined by the Hierarchy
PHYSICAL OUTPUT
Evolving solutions that remain cognitively consistent because of your lens
A GRILL CAN ADOPT PRODUCTION AND LOGISTICS PRACTICES TO DRIVE DOWN COSTS AND SPEED UP TURN TIMES TO BECOME A LOWEST COST, HIGHEST VOLUME PROVIDER.
PHYSIOLOGICAL NEEDS BY BEING THE MOST CONVENIENT, FASTEST SERVING MEAL WHEN YOU NEED TO EAT NOW.
+
INCOME SAFETY NEEDS BY BEING THE LOWEST COST PROVIDER.
PHYSIOLOGICAL SOLUTIONS
- CONVENIENT LOCATIONS EVERYWHERE.
- FASTEST ORDERING AND PRODUCTION TIMES WHEN YOU ARE THERE.
- SATIATING MEALS.
INCOME SAFETY SOLUTIONS
- ASSEMBLY LINE PRACTICES ON SITE
- GLOBAL LOGISTICS TO KEEP COSTS LOW
- TECHNOLOGY INVESTMENTS TO DRIVE SCALE AT LOWER COSTS THAN OTHERS, KEEPING PRICING AT LOWEST IN MARKET.
Source: Peter LeSar

Study McDonald's Concept Architecture just as I walked you through Noma's. The clockwise rotation from the starting line makes it easy to unwrap how McDonald's concept came to be. It's not a static hamburger QSR concept at all, is it? Rather it has a wonderfully fluid concept guard railed by the truths it pursues and the needs it solves. McDonald's success stems from its flexibility to adjust with the times in a way that feels cognitively consistent to the market.

Now, let's follow up on my previous claim. Could McDonald's thrive if it didn't serve hamburgers? The answer can be found in India where even though *serving beef is illegal*, McDonald's is this billion-person market's largest to fourth largest chain depending on whose data you believe. Because McDonald's concept is not "hamburger QSR", it has done extraordinarily well even in markets where beef consumption is illegal or culturally less acceptable. McDonald's is the world's largest restaurant business because its concept is flexible and resilient enough for it to adjust to the ever-changing conditions of the world. The correct architecture of your concept is what matters most to your success as well.

HOW DO YOU RESHAPE THE CONCEPT OF AN EXISTING RESTAURANT?

In 2011, Consumer Reports ranked Chipotle as the best Mexican fast-food chain. With Chipotle's fast rise to over 1,000 stores, Taco Bell's future performance was vulnerable. On the next page, see how Taco Bell applied the concept architecture to reformulate its concept starting in 2012, which was 50 years after its founding. This case study shows you how to adjust your concept years after first opening, and the rationale for doing so.

ARCHITECTURE OF TACO BELL'S RESTAURANT CONCEPT

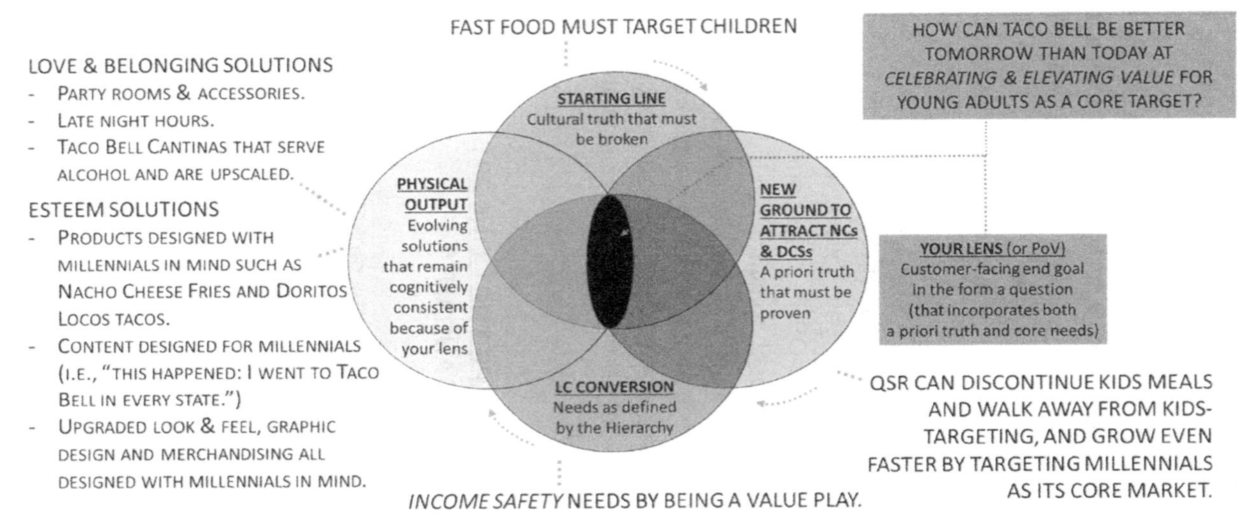

Source: Peter LeSar

Study Taco Bell's Concept Architecture just you like you have those of Noma and McDonald's. Here is the backstory. In 2012, Taco Bell had come off of four years of flat same store sales. The challenge according to then recently instated CEO Greg Creed in a 2019 interview in *Nation's Restaurant News* was that *"the brand wasn't well positioned"* and that *"it wasn't relevant."* These are genuine challenges as you now understand and not just corporate jargon. Creed needed a solution.

In the same year, Taco Bell updated its tagline to *Live Más*, which translates to *Live More*. The tagline update signaled that Taco Bell was re-positioning. Its move reflected a tiny concept adjustment with huge repercussions for Taco Bell's business, which is exactly what you should be looking for in your restaurant.

For Taco Bell, the bilingual tagline broke a cultural truth, which was that a tagline should be communicated in a single language. Taco Bell's opposite a priori truth was that a tagline could reflect its increasingly multi-cultural markets and its position as a bi-cultural brand. This is interesting and would make for great discussion, but there was a second cultural truth around demographics that was less obvious and turned out to be even more powerful.

Taco Bell had observed the cultural truth that fast food restaurants must target children in order to lock in their lifetime values from a young age. It also had observed that its Mexican-inspired food was perceived as more festive than the food of most QSRs *and* that its flavor profiles were bolder and could be less aligned with what parents might prefer to serve to small children. Taco Bell formed an a priori truth to pursue the opposite of QSR's cultural truth, which meant transitioning away from children to pursuing Millennials as their core market as confirmed by Creed in *USA Today* in 2013:

> *"The future of Taco Bell is not about kids' meals. This is about positioning the brand for Millennials."*

Taco Bell's a priori truth was an entirely new approach in the QSR space. It then did what you are supposed to do once your a priori truth is in place. It studied the *needs of its core target* as confirmed by Creed in a QSR Magazine article that same year:

> *"The brand [Taco Bell] isn't a fan of innovating just for the sake of innovating. In reality, its creations and evolutions are largely—if not wholly—driven by deep insights into customers' wants and needs."*

When it looked at the needs of Millennials, Taco Bell discovered that nobody specialized in their *love & belonging* and *esteem* needs within the QSR space. Solving those needs was wide-open territory. Taco Bell understood that teens and young adults are the most festive of all generations and that it could emphasize the celebratory aspects of its offerings and elevate QSR into more of a young adult experience. *Celebrate* and *elevate* value for Millennials became Taco Bell's mantra. It was a narrow path worth leading as Creed himself recognized in *Nation's Restaurant News*:

> *"One of the best things we've done at Taco Bell...is get really focused on the few things that matter and then stay after them."*

Taco Bell began innovating through its new lens as summarized in its architecture above, and it began to attract many more Millennial NCs and DCs who it then converted in to larger numbers of LCs. Taco Bell went from four years of almost nil same store growth to adding $320 thousand of additional same store revenue. What was a major factor in Taco Bell's success? Again, Creed in QSR in 2018:

> *"Taco Bell....proudly stands in a category of one."*

Taco Bell framed a category with all of the financial benefits that clear category leadership provides. It made a tiny concept adjustment (customer-facing end goal as a question) that gifted

Taco Bell its own innovation path. It followed the architecture above just like you are capable of doing if you just *get your hands dirty* into the process.[106] In summary on this point:

> **Insight #67: To shift your concept into a high-performing one does *not* require that you change your current food, format or ambiance at all. What it means is that every innovation you launch must move you toward your new customer-facing end goal.**

You can use this concept architecture to move step-by-step from where you are today to where you need to go. Now, please see again the *Restaurant Growth Model* below as shared with you in Chapter 1. We have now thoroughly reviewed Step 1 and Step 1 (continued). I will now unveil Step 2, which will clearly lay out for you the nuts & bolts of how you grow.

---

106 Remember that defining and leading your category is how most of the income and wealth are generated in the restaurant industry.

RESTAURANT GROWTH MODEL™

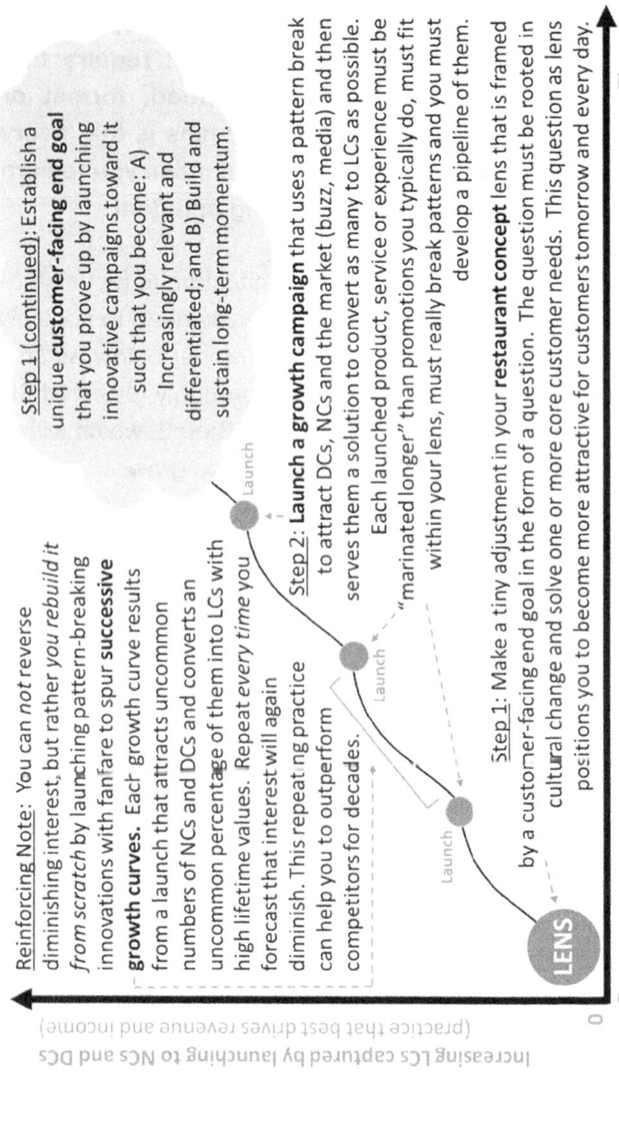

Increasing LCs captured by launching to NCs and DCs (practice that best drives revenue and income)

Reinforcing Note: You can *not* reverse diminishing interest, but rather *you rebuild it from scratch* by launching pattern-breaking innovations with fanfare to spur **successive growth curves.** Each growth curve results from a launch that attracts uncommon numbers of NCs and DCs and converts an uncommon percentage of them into LCs with high lifetime values. Repeat *every time* you forecast that interest will again diminish. This repeating practice can help you to outperform competitors for decades.

Step 1 (continued): Establish a unique **customer-facing end goal** that you prove up by launching innovative campaigns toward it such that you become: A) Increasingly relevant and differentiated; and B) Build and sustain long-term momentum.

Launch

Step 2: **Launch a growth campaign** that uses a pattern break to attract DCs, NCs and the market (buzz, media) and then serves them a solution to convert as many to LCs as possible. Each launched product, service or experience must be "marinated longer" than promotions you typically do, must fit within your lens, must really break patterns and you must develop a pipeline of them.

Launch

Launch

Step 1: Make a tiny adjustment in your **restaurant concept** lens that is framed by a customer-facing end goal in the form of a question. The question must be rooted in cultural change and solve one or more core customer needs. This question as lens positions you to become more attractive for customers tomorrow and every day.

LENS

0

Day one

Time

Source: Peter LeSar

STEP 2 - OUR LAUNCH FRAMEWORK

I start below by *showing you something breathtaking*. Then we will move on to the growth campaign building process. When implemented with genuine effort, the steps ahead offer restaurant companies the best probability of achieving their big, unspoken financial goals. Enjoy these pages...you deserve them and the benefits they can bring.

In the chapter on A Priori Principle I wrote:

> *...if you can't juxtapose yourself from the patterns that people experience in their everyday lives, and then do it again and again, you will fail to be noticed to the extent required to drive extraordinary financial outcomes.*

I have intentionally spoken to patterns and pattern breaks from the start of this book so as to lock them into your conscious mind. I then wrote:

> *Without such an approach, you essentially guarantee that you will just be one more gazelle among thousands. Pretty. Graceful perhaps. But blended in among all except for those few restaurants that are like tiger roars in a silent forest.*

You likely recall my use of the words "gazelle" and "tiger roars". Why would you remember those three words when you read them *tens of thousands of words ago*? To make the point, let me give you a few other examples:

- If you were to see a bright red apple sitting in a bin among one hundred bright green ones, which one apple would stand out? *The red one, but why is that?*
- Have you noticed that the stories you tell from your childhood are all about *uncommon* experiences? You don't share the common and mundane when you want to excite and connect with people. *Why is that and what is so incredibly important about the uncommon?*

- Think about how both historical events and visionary leaders tend to lead us away from an aging, faltering view of the world to a better & brighter one. *Why are events and people that bring about transitions so large in our collective mindset?*

This book has been laying the groundwork for what I am about to say. Breathe for a moment and read this slowly:

- Each of your to-be-launched products, services and/or experiences must be a *red apple* against a bin of green ones—you sell out by standing alone.
- Your restaurant must tell us a continuing story of its *uncommon journey*—this is how you engage us for years and even decades on end.
- Your restaurant's truth must mark and show us a *transition* from a fading world to a better one—this is how you become unbeatable.

The three approaches above are pattern breaks that play to different levels of the human experience and psyche. When you deliver on any of the three, you grow. When you gift yourself all of them, you win. Pattern breaks leverage a psychological phenomenon known as the "isolation effect" that, as described by University of North Carolina Professor R. Reed Hunt in the *Psychonomic Bulletin & Review*, works as follows:

> *"If all but one item of a list are similar on some dimension, memory for the different item will be enhanced."*

The isolation effect was first uncovered by German psychologist Hedwig Von Restorff in 1933 when studies she performed showed that our brains tend not to notice nor recall the common *in order to reserve our energy to notice and recall the uncommon*. Uncommon words, colors, personal stories, facial features, names, historical moments, products, advertisements, art, restaurants, people, hairstyles, humor, personalities and life moments all alert us to look at them as a biological response to protect ourselves and then, because they are different, to later recall them with more ease as they don't fit into any easy frameworks. The isolation effect is the underlying condition that makes juxtaposition so powerful because it makes us see what is unique. We notice the:

- Red apple because it rests in the bin of green ones.
- Uncommon story because of the common ones.
- Transitional moments and figures, because most moments and people have little impact.

Restaurants that leverage the isolation effect in the ways discussed are *always seen and recalled* and those that do not are usually ignored and easily forgotten.

Insight #68: The isolation effect is the most important psychological bias underlying the gap between ordinary and extraordinary outcomes in the restaurant business because its use promotes visibility and recall.

We need to be different in order to be seen and recalled, and the more different we are the more we are seen and recalled. There are vast amounts of income being made or lost in that sentence, depending on where you are on that continuum. Here is what makes being different a relatively easy achievement:

The modern reading of the isolation effect does not require that something is different from everything else, but simply <u>different given the context</u>.

As long as you do something that contrasts greatly within your niche, your community and/or your culture, there are countless opportunities for you to become a red apple who stands brightly out from all of the green ones. Here is how a few category leaders chose to be different given the context of their times, and how they became *changemakers* as a result:

- McDonald's chose to be different in how they built burgers, and they changed the world to one that could consume on the go.
- El Bulli chose to be different in that it deconstructed traditional recipes, and inspired chefs everywhere to transition to deconstructivism as a means of modernizing the traditional cuisines of their own markets.
- Momofuku Noodle Bar chose to be different in showing that the ethnic and cultural roots of all Americans should also be considered integral to American cuisine, transforming our understanding of who should be celebrated in our culinary culture.

Here are examples of how category leaders leveraged the isolation effect to elevate their brands:

- *Brand assets*: Ronald McDonald is a clown who wouldn't have stood out at a circus, but as a brand asset deviated from the norms of the 1960s and made McDonald's more recallable. TGI Friday's tiffany lamps and drinks with umbrellas were unique brand assets for a bar of the 1960s in New York City, but they made TGI Friday's visible and recallable, spurring its early growth. Chipotle's *real food* language in a fast segment stood isolated and apart from its fast-food competitors, and quickly elevated the young brand's profile to a national one in the 1990s. IHOP changing its name temporarily to IHOB in the 2010s, The French Laundry's use of a wooden clothes pin in its publications and hundreds of other examples are all powerful *red apple* brand assets *designed from the get go to stand out*. Their developers observed what competitors were doing, chose to move in a near opposite direction and then trademarked names, logos, icons and slogans to protect the visibility and recall-ability those breaks in patterns provided. Category leaders use their trademarked assets all of the time and spend even hundreds of millions of dollars to put them in front of us so that we visualize who they are in *isolation to everyone else*.[107]

- *Restaurant owner personal branding*: An owner's personal brand assets also leverage the isolation effect, as seen in Guy Fieri's dyed yellow hair, Gordon Ramsey's bluntness, Paul Prudhomme's beret, Slutty Vegan founder's name Pinky Cole and Colonel Sanders' white suit. But brand assets go beyond physical attributes or personality or gimmicks. Thought leadership speaks to ideas that are out of context for restaurateurs in order to make them more visible and recallable. Founders' origin stories are true, but story themes are prioritized to isolate in our minds the uncommon rationale for their brand's existence. The flip side is that your sameness in look, personality, what you speak to and the stories you tell about your restaurant are incalculable penalties on your growth rate and income potential. You must fix this. Figure out what your unique brand assets are or could be, strengthen them and grow. Juxtapose them against the brand assets of others, and grow even more.

Watered-down isolation (green apples versus yellow ones) won't turn the heads of NCs and DCs which, painful as it sounds, is why your growth rate of NC and DC arrivals has likely tapered over the years. If you commit to pattern breaks as a practice, you can develop an uncommon ability to lift ever-higher the visibility of and recall for your restaurant, and to permanently reverse that tapering. Let's see how this works. The Step 2 phases below all refer to the "Step 2: Launch a Growth

---

[107] The isolation effect is also important in restaurant naming. Momofuku and Fuku, two of David Chang's restaurant brands, were intentionally named to break patterns so that you notice them. So was highly medi-agenic Slutty Vegan that became a standout brand during Covid-19.

Campaign" from the Restaurant Growth Model diagram above, which I recommend you review again briefly before diving in.

STEP 2, PHASE A[108] – INNOVATE A PATTERN-BREAKING PRODUCT

Every restaurant needs two types of products: those that LCs return for time and again and that build profits, and those that turn NC and DC heads because you have isolated them in some way from all of the products of your competition. A few products can do both and become powerful business builders, but the best way to find those products is through smaller innovations that unfold more remarkable ones. Products can be pattern-breaking in many ways, including in: name, ingredients, technique, presentation, marketing and context.

In-n-out Burgers' "Double Double Animal Style Burger" is a product name that uses the isolation effect wonderfully. Wendy's "Baconator" is another. Happy Meal boxes and Chipotle's foil-wrapped burritos are examples of the isolation effect in presentation as is Thomas Keller's White Truffle Oil Infused Custard served in an egg shell, which as a photo has been viewed by countless foodies around the world. The very goal of molecular gastronomy, as used in Alinea's edible balloon, is to break the pattern of recipes altogether as is the practice of deconstructivism. Burger King's flame-grilled is a technique used to juxtapose and stand isolated against McDonald's electric grills. When you name products in common styles and use common words, when you use common packaging and plating, and

[108] Large pattern breaks are usually uncovered from the observations and data you gather from small ones. In other words, *we peel back big wins by diving deeper on the impact of small ones*. You can undertake the steps below without ever having made the tiny adjustment (customer-facing end goal as a question) in your concept. The results over time will be far better if you do, but I have clients who have started with Step 2 and who come back to concept positioning later. You decide where to make your first move.

when you fail to access uncommon ingredients, you ignore the isolation effect as the most important tool for driving NCs and DCs to look at you, recall you and come to dine with you. You reduce your growth prospects.

Insight #69: Pattern-breaking products are a growth multiplier because they inspire more customers (sometimes many multiples more) to show up as compared to products that don't break patterns.

Your first job is to develop a product using the isolation effect, meaning that you want to find the opposite or near opposite from an existing pattern as much as possible.[109]

Product development case study: When Papa John's wanted to improve its day-part business, it observed pizza competitors and saw that they served calzones to promote lunch sales. When it looked at non-pizza restaurants that competed in its price point, Papa John's saw its customers going to sub shops. The competitor patterns at lunchtime were calzones and subs. Staying with the pattern would not excite NCs or DCs who would need a reason to change habits to Papa John's. Papa John's needed to break from calzones and subs, but still wanted its new product to be handheld because portability solves many

[109] To communicate pattern breaks requires that you identify its differentiated values. For example, Burger King juxtaposed its use of sourdough in breakfast sandwiches by asking itself component-level questions such as: How is the taste different? How does it feel or smell differently? And, why is it better for you in health, price, size, presentation and do so on as compared to the options offered by competitors? If you don't create a powerful frame for your products, no one will.

customer needs.[110] The closest it could find to an opposite was to innovate Papadias, which are open-faced sandwiches made of pizza bread, but less doughy than closed-faced calzones and with flavor profiles that are not calzone-like such as Philly Cheese Steak Papadias, Grilled Buffalo Chicken Papadias and BBQ Chicken Bacon Papadias. Papadias, a brand new, pattern-breaking product category, were launched and within months propelled Papa John's to its best revenue month ever, as acknowledged in *Restaurant Business* at the time:

> *"A lot of the growth is coming from the chain's new sandwich product, Papadias, introduced earlier this year. <u>It has generated lunch business for the chain and incremental sales.</u>"*[111, 112]

Design a pattern-breaking product: Here is how you do this: A) List each small component of a pattern you find. For example, if competitors serve a side salad to their steak entrées, write down the size and ingredients of the salad and how it is presented. In its own component-level observations, Papa John's will have observed that calzones were closed-faced and that the opposite of that would be an open-faced sandwich also made with pizza dough. B) Do what Papa John's did and take note of

---

110 Portable food serves any number of human needs such as: A) Physiological need that "I need fresh air and sun shine after being cooped up in an office"—handheld lunches are easier to eat any place outside as compared to a plated meal that requires utensils and a flat surface; B) Love & belonging, because again its portability makes it easier to carry and eat alongside a friend or loved one on a lunch break; and C) Income or job safety, because handheld food is faster to consume than plated food, and just a better solution for when "I need to eat something quick and keep working at my desk" on whatever rush job is due that next hour or that day.

111 Again, it is typical for a product launch to add to incremental sales of other products.

112 Ideally you want each product you launch to not just turn heads because it is pattern breaking, but to actually be your best possible products. A big goal of product development is when, like with Papadias, you find a platform food that serves needs you currently don't serve.

what is the opposite or near opposite of each component, and brainstorm on them. Following our example, the simple opposite of a large steak entre and small green dinner salad would be a small steak entre with a large salad. When you think that through, it might seem likely to you that lighter eaters (focused on health) and lower-budget customers (focused on income safety) might respond to a small steak, large salad pattern break. You could then take that a step forward and design a series of larger salads that customers can "pair" with their steak, using flavor profile language in the style of how a sommelier might describe a pairing of a meal with wine. The goal would be to entice NCs and DCs to return to try other pairings. You want to do as much brainstorming as is reasonable for each component or components in combination, always stretching for as close to an opposite and (for your target customer) a best-solution way forward. Write down all of your ideas and then choose the one that would least impact on operations, would most make you look twice in surprise and that builds you toward your customer-facing end goal (if you have one).

Design your product name: Your pattern breaking must extend to how you name the product, service or experience. Here are rules to product naming that category leaders follow:

- Name it what it is.
- Use words that are unique or even made up.
- Put the pattern break in the name.

A Papa*dia* translates from Spanish to Papa "day" and is Papa John's made-up word for saying that its product was intended for day-part consumption. Papa John's nailed two of the rules, and that was enough. Other segments use the same naming approach but use language that is appropriate for their category. Blue Hill at Stone Barns *Grazing, Pecking, Rooting* menu complies with all three naming rules above.

Design your marketing language: Your pattern breaking must extend to how you message about the product, service or experience. There are four rules to marketing language that category leaders follow as per the below that includes Papadia's marketing language as real examples:

- Tell your market what your product, service or experience being launched is *not*, so that consumers understand the pattern you are breaking: *"Papadia isn't just any flatbread sandwich".*[xxvi]
- With specificity, tell your market how delicious your product is, with an emphasis on its standout, component-level traits: *"Think real cheese melted to perfection, juicy meats, and mountains of colorful veggies, all nestled snugly into fresh-baked flatbread made from Papa John's own signature dough."*
- Tell your market how your product serves life moments: *"Makes ideal finishing touches to any pizza order for a party, a family dinner, or even just a low-key Saturday night at home, as well as great ways to dress up an otherwise humdrum lunch hour!"*
- After doing all of the above, come up with a tagline. Even if your restaurant doesn't use taglines, they are great in-house tools for staff to communicate the essence of the product to customers. Your tagline should capture the needs served so that people have easy clarity as to why to consume the product, service or experience being launched. Papadias' tagline as a handheld meal that is consumed at lunch, at parties and as a dinner side is: *"Portable deliciousness for any occasion."*

Preparing this language in advance of a launch prepares you to maximize NC and DC visits. If you don't create and share the pattern-breaking frame for the market, few will realize that you have broken a pattern at all and your launch will be less effective. Your don't have to be perfect. Get it done, get it out, learn and keep getting better as a practice.

STEP 2, PHASE B - LAUNCH YOUR PRODUCT

Thought leadership worked in our restaurants because it lifted our market to a global one, but also intensified the discussions about us within our neighborhoods. Thought leadership is a rising tide that permanently lifts your brand, but unlike launches, it can take years to work on and for the word to get out.

Launches are also growth multipliers, but in a different way. Launches are an explosion of fireworks and then they are gone. They turn people intensely toward you for a short period of time, but have the same goal as thought leadership—to attract larger numbers of NCs and DCs than you otherwise can and convert larger numbers of LCs as a result.

Non-category leaders often try launches and drop them as a practice because they don't seem to work. To understand why that is the case, answer this question for yourself:

What is the purpose of a launch?

Most restaurant professionals answer more or less as follows: *"The purpose of a launch is to let people know about something new or something that has changed."*

This answer is akin to saying you score points in basketball by putting the ball in the hoop. Technically it's correct, but a seasoned player would not answer this way. She would talk about the execution of set plays, of offensive and defensive strategy, of game awareness and team collaboration. All of these must come together to earn points in competitive leagues and *restaurants are a sort of competitive league*. When I hear a generic answer to the "purpose of a launch" question, I know that a restaurant is not competing effectively.

So how do you make launches work incredibly well to produce revenue growth?

Fireworks bring crowds because they offer a short pattern break in our lives. Likewise, pattern-breaking launches attract crowds far better than your normal diluted marketing practices do. When you opened, it was a launch of sorts and it worked like fireworks. You were new, pattern-breaking and people came in to see what was going on. When your initial novelty wore off and your growth curve flattened, you needed a new round of fireworks. I told you at the beginning of this book that "what category leaders do to beat the inevitable flattening of revenue is not to extend their original growth curve, but to build *many new growth curves*." Launches ignite those growth curves because, when executed as per this section, they:

- Concentrate pattern-breaking characteristics (ingredients, technique, plating, naming, background story) into a new product, service or experience launch;
- Concentrate pattern-breaking marketing during a concentrated time frame to a highly targeted NC & DC customer type;
- Market at a greater scale than you do now, so that you can properly leverage all of the preparation it takes to do the above; and
- Leverage time scarcity to drive NCs and DCs in before they lose out on being able to experience something valuable for them—just like fireworks do.

Your launch assets, when deployed as per the guidelines of the Growth Model, make the market look at you actively rather than passively, and the increased attention starts a new growth curve. Below is diagram showing how launches act as a growth multiplier. Note that the diagram is a zoomed-in look at Step 2 from our Restaurant Business Model diagram, but now with a critical clarification.

THE ROLE OF LAUNCHES

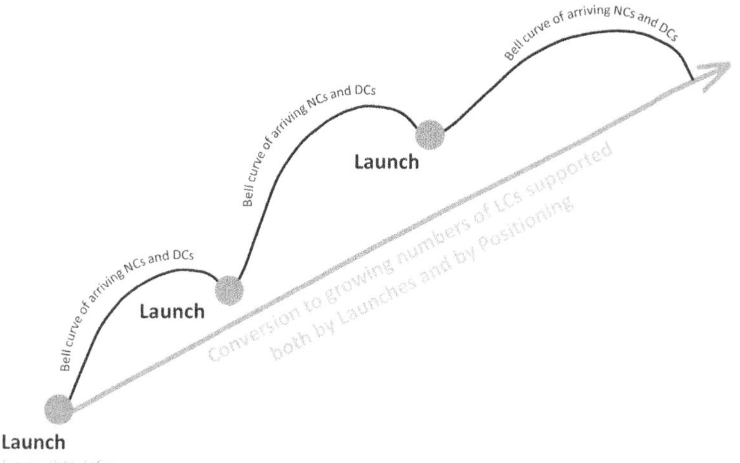

Every category leader sets its own pace of launches, with the goal of each to *reignite interest* from NCs, DCs and to stack up more LC lifetime values to reset revenue another notch higher with each launch. This is key, so pay attention:

- When you do a normal promotion and attract only LCs, you produce a revenue bump from their additional visits, but produce no change in your revenue trajectory.
- On the other hand, when you use launches to target NCs and DCs and when you improve your solutions as your operating strategy, your revenues don't bump up only during some short promotional period, but reset at a higher level because new LCs are stacked on top of your existing ones every time.
- As the interest in each product launch wanes, category leaders launch whatever next pattern break they have in the development pipeline in order to notch their revenue up again. They repeat this practice forever. It's how they grow faster and go farther than you.

When you see Taco Bell launch nine products a year, they are using launches in the form of limited-time offers to notch up their revenue. When you see The French Laundry launch a new $10 million kitchen *that millions hear about*, they are also doing a launch to achieve the exact outcome that Taco Bell does with its LTOs: attract more NCs and DCs to then stack up more LCs and their high-dollar LTVs. You don't usually notice the product launch strategy because each category leader's pacing and launch mechanics are distinct based on its type of restaurant.

On one side of the restaurant continuum:

Insight #70: Destination fine dining restaurants with their high price points and limited seating tend to launch deeply planned-out menu change-ups 2-4 times a year *and* experience upgrades every 3-7 years as that is the two-part strategy required to attract the number of NCs and DCs they need to hit and sustain their LC conversion and revenue growth rate targets.

Such is the case with the launch of Noma's three seasons of menus (seafood, vegetable and game), which are LTOs using higher-brow narratives and language to attract free media to help them to get the word out. Such was also the case with Noma 1.0 versus Noma 2.0 that focused on its infrastructure and experience upgrade. In this latter case, Noma fully invested its media power to help it to quickly amortize and earn a high return from its infrastructure investment. The greater the risk you take in your launches, the more you need to power the frame of the pattern break itself, which is your best practice for mitigating risk and maximizing return.

On the other side of the continuum:

Insight #71: Fast food restaurants with their low-pricing, high-volume models launch 4-9

> **LTOs a year to attract the number of NCs and DCs required to hit their LC conversion and revenue growth rate targets.**[113]

Some LTOs can monumentally shift revenues up as was the case with Popeye's spicy chicken sandwich LTO that single-handedly added an average of $400 thousand of sales per year to each of its thousands of stores. Other LTOs generate smaller revenue resets—as was the case with Burger King's Impossible Burger that raised revenues as compared to the previous quarter—and then require more rapid-fire LTOs to keep building their momentum.

Well-planned launches change outcomes, but:

> **Insight #72: Even mediocre launches build future income more effectively than other types of marketing because they attract NCs and DCs in volumes *as their primary objective*. Marketing objectives matter greatly to bottom line results.**

What you likely do today is scatter multiple offers around simultaneously and with no real fanfare. Your approach is diluted and relatively ineffectual at attracting NCs and DCs because it wasn't designed with that outcome in mind.

Launches, on the other hand, are bursts of exposure that stack up many $2400-lifetime-spending LCs or whatever LTV number produced by your average LC.[114] The result of regularly scheduled, pattern-breaking launches is that you wake up tomorrow knowing that your minimum revenue will be X and in

[113] The pace and intensity of launches done by category leaders in other segments tends to fall somewhere between these two extremes.

[114] The supplemental materials include an Excel sheet to help you to calculate LTV.

three months it will be predictably higher than X as you stack up more LCs—as shown in *The Role of Launches* above.

Below are the tables we studied in Chapter 3 to understand the gross profit impact of a 10% versus a 15% conversion rate of NCs and DCs to LCs. Highlighted near the top of the left base case table is the number *100*, estimating the number of NCs and DCs generated in a month without a pattern-breaking launch ongoing. Highlighted in the table on the right is the number *200*, estimating that the number of NC and DC arrivals will double during a launch period. Please note the 300% increase in gross profits generated by doubling your NC and DC arrivals from your same marketing spend, now focused on a launch vs. a more diluted approach. *That is the forecasted spread from one launch and from one month of marketing.*

BASE CASE RESTAURANT 10-YEAR RETURN BASED ON *10%* LC CONVERSION RATE (all else being equal and after 1 month of marketing spend)		
MARKETING SPEND IN A MONTH	$	1,000
NCs & DCs GENERATED IN SAME MONTH		100
CONVERSION RATE TO LC		10%
LCs GENERATED IN SAME MONTH		10
AVERAGE TICKET PER CUSTOMER	$	20
VISITS PER MONTH PER AVERAGE LC		1
LIFETIME TERM (IN MONTHS)		120
NC & DC REVENUE GENERATED IN MONTH	$	2,000
LC REVENUE GENERATED OVER THEIR LIFETIME	$	24,000
ADDED REVENUE FROM ONE MONTH MARKETING	$	26,000
COST OF GOODS SOLD		30%
10-YEAR GROSS PROFIT FROM MARKETING SPEND	$	18,226
RETURN ON MARKETING SPEND		1823%

Source: Peter LeSar

HIGHER GROWTH RESTAURANT 10-YEAR RETURN BASED ON *15%* LC CONVERSION RATE + LEVERAGING LAUNCHES TO GROW (all else being equal and after 1 month of marketing spend)		
MARKETING SPEND IN A MONTH	$	1,000
NCs & DCs GENERATED IN SAME MONTH		200
CONVERSION RATE TO LC		15%
LCs GENERATED IN SAME MONTH		30
AVERAGE TICKET PER CUSTOMER	$	20
VISITS PER MONTH PER AVERAGE LC		1
LIFETIME TERM (IN MONTHS)		120
NC & DC REVENUE GENERATED IN MONTH	$	4,000
LC REVENUE GENERATED OVER THEIR LIFETIME	$	72,000
ADDED REVENUE FROM ONE MONTH MARKETING	$	76,000
COST OF GOODS SOLD		30%
10-YEAR GROSS PROFIT FROM MARKETING SPEND	$	53,276
RETURN ON MARKETING SPEND		5328%

Source: Peter LeSar

What would happen if every month for a year was a launch month with these same assumptions?[115] You would add $638 thousand of growth profit over 10 years as compared to our base case, which translates to an additional $5,300 of gross profit per month

[115] You can expect perhaps 1 out of every 10 launches to hit such a sweet spot that its effect is a multiple of even the standard multiplier performance of a launch-based growth practice.

for a decade.[116] This is the power of well-structured launches and *is how our leaders nuts & bolts build revenue and income.*

To optimize NC-DC traffic and LC conversions, you should add the following steps to your launches:

Define all purposes: Define all other purposes of the launch.

- *Are you trying to attract a higher-spending clientele?* If so, your product or service to be launched should pursue a quality-up, price-up approach. The whole fast casual category was built off of this strategy in juxtaposition to fast food. Destination fine dining has likewise moved farther and farther up the quality-price ladder to appeal to gastro-tourist jet setters.
- *Are you trying to increase both margins and LC conversions?* If so, you could stretch for a quality-up, cost-down approach. This takes creativity, but produces the highest returns on advertising when taking into account LTVs. Casual family dining with its thin margins and rising competition from fast casual has made quality up, cost down a build-back strategy to convert more LCs from the NCs and DCs that show up.
- *Are you trying to offer better value-for-money than you do today?* If so, you can try a price down, volume up approach. This approach led McDonald's same store growth for decades (by enticing customers with the lowest prices and then incentivizing upsizing).

The above are not the only purposes you might consider in your launches. Here are a few others among countless possibilities: *Do you want to target a local hospital's staff or a local university's students? Do you wish to grow your happy hour or*

[116] The math is: (($53,200 of future revenue created from LCs based on 1 month of launch marketing) X (12 months of launch marketing)) / (120 months of the lifetime of the average customer). In the worksheets made available to you, you can build your own estimates and change such factors as lifetime term, average ticket, visits per month, LC conversion rate and so on to tailor this and our other forecasts to your own business.

late-night dining? Do you want to attract larger table sizes? Do you want to reduce your hours of operation, but earn more per hour? You need to first list your core launch goals for each individual launch, and then make sure that whatever you launch is targeted to achieve those goals.

As context for the remaining launch steps, see this quote from Chef Carla Hall:[117]

"The biggest challenge of being a pastry chef is that, unlike other types of chefs, you can't throw things together at a farmer's market. When you're working with baking powder and a formula, you have to be exact. If not, things can go wrong."[xxvii]

Ignore launch formulas, and your restaurant won't rise much. This has always been the case. Advances in technology have not altered the underlying approach of launches at all, but have made easier the practical details of scaling them up. Regardless of when you put your next launch into effect, the steps below will still apply.

Choose a launch period for your product or service launch. Product and service launch periods should be no less than 30 days, but can be as long as 120 days depending on the type of restaurant you have. I generally recommend 60-90 days. In your advertising, let the market know that your launch has an expiration date and that the product or service will no longer be available after that date. Always try to end the launch on the last calendar day of a month. The idea of all product and service launches is to let them teach you what to do next as the launch period expires, with these options:

- Let it expire and terminate the product or service if it didn't perform well.

[117] Hall first gained renown as a contestant on Bravo's Top Chef. She has since become a culinary star hosting shows and appearing on programs across the media world. I recommend her three cook books.

- Extend the offer for a specific additional period of time if NCs and DCs are still pouring in.
- Or, you can make your product or service a permanent offering because it has also turned into a strong profit center with your loyal customer base.

Your decision on what to do as a launch period nears its end is a financial one. Based on my experience, most launches should be expired because they will have served their purpose, approximately 20% to 30% should be extended for a month or more because they are still contributing to growth, and around 10% to 20% should be made permanent because they are long-term game changers (in which case, you should rotate out products or services that are under performing, so that you are continually renewing the business ever-more narrowly toward answering your customer-facing end-goal of a question).

Choose a launch period for your experience launch: Experience launches are generally about infrastructure investments. Extending your bar, building additional parking, adding breakfast service, bringing on a new type of pizza oven, expanding your outdoor dining areas and so on are all experience-infrastructure improvements that should be launched to more quickly amortize that investment. Experience launches also have time limits on them, but generally announce no expiration date. Because the experience adds value, you should communicate that value effectively by showing how it better solves needs. Experience launch periods are generally 30-60 days but there is a profitable way to extend them out for longer periods. With the added infrastructure, you will uncover new products and services to launch that leverage the infrastructure and experience added. As an example, you can first launch a new bar and then execute on five follow-on launches of new products or services that encourage uncommon levels of bar uptake. Launches start with the infrastructure and continue perhaps forever with how customers can leverage that infrastructure to solve their needs.

Set a budget and measure your launch returns. When everything else is prepared, work on your marketing budget. To optimize marketing the way category leaders do, you must practice *self-liquidating advertising* which is advertising that quickly pays for itself so that you can immediately reinvest to grow. How did McDonald's scale from a tiny ad budget to even a $50-million-dollar-a-month one? With self-liquidating advertising.

Insight #73: Self-liquidating advertising is when your ad spend quickly converts into sales and returns your ad spend and then some, such that you can then increase ad spend for your next launch to generate even more revenue.

The goal is to *roll this process forward for years until your ad spend is a multiple of where it is today, because it has built your revenues into a multiple of where they are today*. Daily ad spend on effective launches are virtually always recouped in gross profit terms within 24 hours. The immediacy and link-ability of the ad spend to gross profit makes performance easy to see.

Since you don't focus your marketing through launches, but in a diffused way, you never had the opportunity to effectively measure your returns on ad spend. When you concentrate your advertising around launches and temporarily halt all other marketing, virtually your entire incremental revenue growth will be directly attributable to your launch campaign. You will be able to link ad spend to revenue and gross profit growth, and to easily measure returns by marketing campaign.

Budgeting for your launch should take into account the benefits of self-liquidating advertising. Start with low numbers (i.e., similar to what you spend on ads today) and increase your spending the deeper you get into the launch as long as you are generating a return on that advertising. The experience of my clients is that throughout a campaign, they generally spend:

- 5% to 15% of revenue on advertising when launch advertising is calculated as a percentage of only the *direct sales of the product or service launched*.
- 1% to 7% when launch advertising is calculated as a percentage of all *incremental revenues during the launch period*. Incremental revenues should be a lot higher than the direct sales of what you launch.[118]
- 0.25% or less when launch advertising is calculated as a percentage of *all lifetime revenue from LCs forecasted to be converted by the launch.*

Here is the point:

> **Insight #74: The return on ad spend that category leaders earn from direct sales of the launched product is usually unattractive. Their return on ad spend when you take into account all incremental sales during the launch period is about on target with industry ratios. On the other hand, when you calculate ad spend as a percentage of LTVs earned from new LCs generated in a campaign, *the returns are off-the-charts attractive even from so-so launches*.**

Your job as said is to advertise to build up your long-term income from LCs, because advertising for short-term gains is a marginal business—today's category leaders became leaders only after they changed their approach. Self-liquidating advertising tied to reinvesting at successively higher levels of ad spend for successively greater levels of future LTV income is what you want for all who are impacted by your business.

---

[118] Launched products and services turn heads when they pattern break, but when customers show up, they *usually* order something other than the product launched and that is just fine.

STEP 2, PHASE C – STACK YOUR LAUNCHES

We will again rely on the *Restaurant Growth Model diagram* in this step, so I include it again for quick reference below (or you can review it in large, full-page format earlier in this chapter).

RESTAURANT GROWTH MODEL

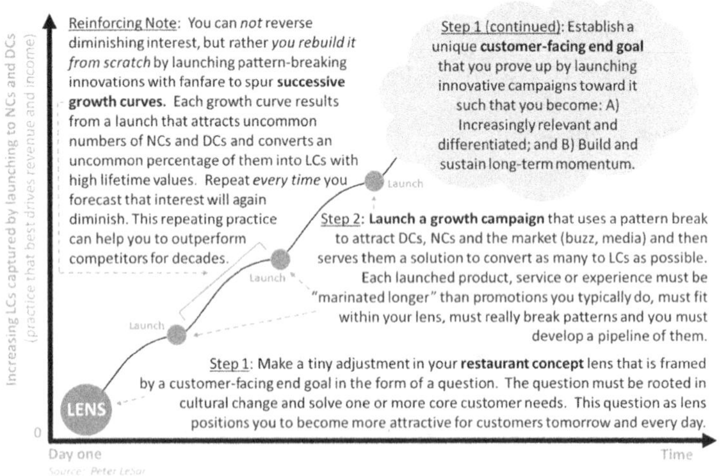

The small dots above represent individual launches. Today's category leaders have executed on dozens to even hundreds of launches depending on what part of the restaurant continuum they work in. You need to define your own launch pace and then to develop a pipeline of pattern-breaking products and services so as one winds down, another can be launched within the pacing you have set. The more months of the year that NCs and DCs experience a launch, the more LC conversions and LTV earnings you will build for your future. The point: there is a huge difference between doing one launch versus many over time, which difference I call "launch stacking".

Did you ever play with Legos? If so, you know that throwing Lego bricks aimlessly around on the floor builds nothing, while stacking them as building blocks is how you create something worthy of your time and effort. Think about a single launch as if it were a single Lego brick. Today, what you likely do is launch a growth campaign around Valentine's Day or Thursday nights or Tuesday lunches, but they are not connected in a way that builds anything. You are scattering your building blocks. You treat them as tools for getting revenue on those days, but not as blocks that you are stacking for the purpose of peeling back more knowledge about what matters to your customers.

What am I saying?

When you launch a product, service or experience, apart from earning revenue and income from the launch, your goal must also be to learn what inspires new customers to visit and what inspires them to convert to loyal ones. Launches provide a concentrated (in both time and number of customer responses) amount of data that more quickly tells you what works and what to fix as compared to your more dilutive marketing. Launches can show you what matters most to customers and to *earn even more as you learn what to do next* with greater clarity.

In other words:

> **Insight #75: Launches are both an earning system *and* a learning system.**

The more you gather insights from the concentration of work and customer responses to a controlled offer, the better you will get at hitting the sweet spot of customer delight the next time around. I see many restaurants that go years without any substantial learning not because they are unable, but because they haven't created the right conditions for learning. An example of the power of launches to provide data is when Popeye's launched its chicken sandwich with a:

- Pattern-breaking buttery brioche bun as standard.
- Pattern-breaking crispiness, including in the pickles.
- Pattern-breaking tweet troll at Chick-fil-A.

If it had behaved like most restaurants, Popeye's would have just placed its sandwich on its menu and hoped people liked it. But because the launch drove huge traffic in a short period, Popeye's was able to observe that its controversy-generating trolling was, among the pattern breaks, the one that most turned the heads of media and of NCs and DCs to give it another chance in what became known as the *chicken sandwich wars.* It was a lesson that Popeye's continues to use and would have otherwise missed.

> **Insight #76: When you only have a customer-facing end goal, you still guess as to what works best because you lack the concentrated data that launches produce.**

I told you earlier that we peel back big wins by diving deeper on the impact of small ones. Launch stacking moves you from small wins to huge ones as it step-by-step unfolds what matters most to your customers, and therefore what works best to grow your business. Below is a concluding scenario that shows how this works in four exciting ways.

Concluding scenario: Let's imagine for a moment that you operate a casual family dining restaurant that is in an area with many young families and small children. The needs of these families under our hierarchy are income safety and love & belonging, meaning they want to save money and to experience quality family time. The cultural truth you have seen in casual family dining a la Applebee's, TGI Friday's, Chili's, Ruby Tuesday's and so on is that they allocate valuable real estate to their bar business. Your a priori truth is that if you allocate that real estate for families to enjoy after-dinner decadent desserts and short games, you will be the best in your market at serving family needs and will more than make up the difference as compared to bar real estate. You found the dessert & game room because you narrowed to this customer-facing end goal in the form of a question: *how can we be better tomorrow than today at creating quality family time at affordable prices (and at attractive returns for stakeholders)?*[119]

Stack needs-focused launches on top of current solutions: Your dessert & game room solution is working. You are turning tables more quickly because fewer families dawdle after their meal, and many move to the more densely seated dessert & game room. You have increased ticket size since more are ordering desserts and paying a small fee to play the games. You have increased family quality time in a way that is frictionless (customers don't have to change venues) at a price that is lower than other post-dinner options such as going to the movies. Now, how can you stack launches to make that dessert & game room solution even more profitable? You could launch post-dinner family trivia night on Tuesdays, which nobody in your market does. You could launch Saturday morning breakfast & babysitting to give parents the space to do errands and/or private offer the room for Saturday afternoon birthday parties. You could launch products designed to attract after-school teen meet ups, mother-son nights and so on. Without the burden of a bar with its limited hours of profitability, you gift yourself an opportunity to build real demand for non-peak hours and days, not just peak ones. Each new use is a pattern-breaking solution that was only possible for you to find *because of an earlier pattern break that you stacked on top of.*

---

[119] If this a priori truth seems silly to you, please note that every a priori truth seems silly until it has been proven. Assembly line kitchens were silly. Bars with tiffany lamps and colorful cocktails were silly. Using real ingredients in fast food was silly for many. Cultural truths are so embedded in the way we think that when we come up with an "opposite" idea, we can quickly back away from it as illogical given that it seems contrary to the way the world works. Herein lies the point: A priori truths are about changing how things work and about uncovering paths to greater growth and larger returns than when you just go with the flow.

Insight #77: Stacking one solution on top of another extends your differentiation to a level that competitors can't readily copy. Stacking innovations is how you differentiate toward category leadership.

Stack a platform of products on top of a current product: Now let's presume that you noticed that parents in the dessert & game room often want to order a drink, but felt it inappropriate both because they were worried about driving and/or because the glassware traditionally used for serving alcohol seemed inappropriate in the kid-focused environment. To address the safety and love & belonging needs inherent in that problem, you launched a low-alcohol margarita in a playful bamboo tiki cup, and mothers who were mostly car passengers really responded. The data from the launch showed you that low-alcohol drinks have legs because they serve a number of *needs,* from customers worrying about driving to those wanting to wake up as their best selves in the morning to those wanting to drink lightly only in order to be social. This led you to develop a *platform of low-alcohol cocktails and spritzers served in celebratory yet safe glassware* (a la the tiki cup) to keep occasions fun in spite of the reduced amount of alcohol. You increased your bar revenue just because you solved more needs than the traditional menu of drinks offered. Moreover, you noticed that serving these drinks in a fun way enabled you to maintain the same pricing as with a standard drink, meaning you hit the trifecta of increasing your sales volume, improving your drink margins and locking in more loyal customers at the same time.

Insight #78: It's easier to uncover a new *platform* food or drink that opens up a new set of needs to serve when you generate a concentrated response from an earlier

pattern-breaking product launch. This is how small pattern breaks snowball into large ones that can play out on many levels.[120]

Stack launches on high-consuming targets: Now let's imagine that you noticed many divorced parents with shared custody showing up for family trivia night. The activity provided something for single parents to do with children that made everyone happy, but you only offer that activity on Tuesday nights. You realize that single parents need more solutions that include fun, intimate, easy-to-participate-in activities for them to enjoy with their kids. You have been thinking about your low occupancy on Sunday late mornings that could feed into lunch and Sunday late afternoons that could feed into early dinner. You decide to invest in paper placemat-based games for all tables in your restaurant that typically last 10-15 minutes per placemat. You also invest in paperback joke books, in trivia cards and in parent-child question & answer cards that are placed in baskets at every table and you relaunch Sundays from 10am to 5pm as Family Love Sundays. You launch parent-child shareable drinks with crazy straws, mix and match chip dips and so on to encourage sharing and easy, fun conversation. You do everything possible to get information about Family Love Sundays in front of single parents who crave low-stress, high-intimacy moments with their children. The market of single parents looking for quality time with their children turns eagerly toward you.

---

120 As a highly visible example, the Shake Shack concept is a huge pattern-breaking opportunity that extended from a small pattern-breaking hot dog stand in Madison Park in New York City, which itself evolved in part out of pattern breaks uncovered in Eleven Madison Park, which in itself evolved in part out of pattern breaks in Union Square Café—all developed by Danny Meyer. Part of Meyer's genius comes from understanding how one innovation points to another that points to another.

Insight #79: Discovering a specific customer behavior from observations made during a launch can open up an entirely new market with its own unique needs.

Stack launches into business expansions: Finally, let's imagine that all of the above has made you the most important restaurant in your market for serving families with elementary and middle school aged children. You have developed narrow solutions with clear competitive advantages that you have converted into sales volume and increased profitability. You have become an expert on this target market and on how to innovate to increase your momentum with it. This is the sort of business that can expand its hours, its table area and maybe even its number of units. This is the sort of business that capital chases, and it's all because you wed your customer-facing end goal to high-data producing launches that taught you what works, what doesn't and shows you how to innovate to keep moving your concept, your category and your financial performance ever farther beyond those of your competitors who failed to grasp the true Restaurant Growth Model *as you now have.*

Is that clear? Now, *you* just need one more lesson. The Epilogue shows you how to **transform your team into an unusually high-growth unit.**

EPILOGUE

WHERE DO YOU START?

How to transform your team into a high-growth unit.

ROY CHOI OF KOGI BBQ food truck fame has said:

"I'm not afraid to do whatever I need to do to keep the food evolving."[xxviii]

In the restaurant business, we do what it takes, right? We are warriors in that sense, trying to care for our customers, our team members and our business all while time seems to get away from us, whether we run a large organization or a small one. The epilogue answers this final, most relevant of questions:

How do you have it all?

Let's dig deep one final time.

TIME-BASED DEVELOPMENT SPRINTS

A root growth challenge for restaurants is what I call the "Moving Parts Continuum." Fast food scales easiest because, in part, it is the most automated and has the least moving parts in its operations. Fine dining scales the least, in part, because it has the most moving parts in both back and front of the house. There is a continuum of complexity in our industry, and even hyper-streamlined fast food is more complex than many other types of businesses.

So many moving parts requires that your company focus foremost on assuring that *today's* customers are served to the standards they expect.

That is healthy, normalized prioritization for a restaurant business, but it is also defensive posturing that impedes great financial outcomes unless you make a critical adjustment.

Insight #80: In your defensive work to solve today's risks to customer satisfaction, you have trouble equally prioritizing the *offense* required to forever lift your growth trajectory.

We prioritize the short-term taking care of loyal customers because our fear of losing them far outweighs the positive feelings we derive from attracting NCs and DCs, which ironically is what we need to build more LCs in the first place. Or, as taken one step further in the *Harvard Business Review*, our:

"Tendency to prefer avoiding losses over achieving equivalent gains drives powerful risk-averse behaviors that can hold us in place like gravity."

Your response to the above might be: "Peter, we have to take care of our customers or we won't have any." My most heart-felt response to you: "It's time to break you free."

Please start by accepting that unsatisfactory results are likely permanent for those restaurant companies that don't steadily increase the time that their senior and department leaders (kitchen, bar, front of house, finance / accounting, HR and marketing) allocate to growth. In beautiful virtuous cycle:

Insight #81: The more time your team aligns around an outperforming growth practice, the more your business grows *and* the more team members will live their best lives.

Ironically, you have to program distinct windows of time first to grow, in order for growth to then gift your team added time, mindspace and financial security for living. That is the order of things. Read the following from David Chang in the *Art of Science* blog, and let's dive in to its underlying message:

> *The Momofuku Culinary Lab started as a space where we could focus on creating and innovating. I didn't want us to worry about working on projects in a restaurant; there are just too many distractions in service and running a kitchen to be able to focus on creating your dishes.*

The point: Like water and ice, operations and growth practice can't co-exist in the same space and time if you want to advance from normal levels of business growth and life rewards to outperforming ones. All category leaders had to learn this to emerge as leaders in the first place. So what do you do?

> **Insight #82: Once you have defined your customer-facing end goal of a question, your next step is to set an aggressive 90-day development goal that gifts you a first sprint in that direction.**

A restaurant not paced by 90-day development cycles is a business waiting to be outcompeted. Category leaders—the 3% of brands that rise above their markets—do not wait for inspiration or fear or market shifts to act; they build strategic urgency into their senior team's culture (and then steadily down the hierarchy) by locking into ever-repeating, time-boxed development sprints. Why? Because restaurant outperformance must be engineered. The longer the delay between bold moves, the more your momentum decays and your relevance fades. High-growth brands treat 90 days as a metronome of innovation—launching products, advancing toward their positioning goals (customer-facing end goals), and training their teams to advance in tight, purposeful sprints.

Insight #83: Successive development sprints that navigate to your customer-facing end goal build those higher rates of revenue growth that are necessary to emerge as a category leader. Once your first 90-day development period is over, document what worked and what didn't, reset the 90-day timer with new aggressive goals, and repeat. Forever.

As you repeat 90-day sprints and advance on your objectives, pay attention to the areas of new expertise that your speed and direction require. Then ask each sprint team member to develop greater expertise in an area that matches their *sui generis* interests and talents.

Insight #84: The greater the expertise each sprint team member develops, the faster and higher the 90-day sprints will drive up business outcomes *and* the quality of life of those who contribute to them.

When I divide the number of LCs our restaurant clients onboard each month by the number of hours their team members spend on growth, the rule of thumb is that they generate one new LC per each hour invested. I want you to imagine that each hour you spend on growth will generate one new LC. If the average LTV of your LCs is $2400 as per our earlier scenario, that would mean your work is valued at $2400 per hour, which is higher than most can charge in any profession. And, this leads us to one final, but mission-critical insight:

Insight #85: Building great financial and life outcomes requires that your team evolve into the highest performing unit *as compared to all competitors*. Therefore, you must forever strengthen the processes and outcomes of your 90-day development sprints, and the team (in talent, dedication and sheer numbers) that contribute to them.

Having it all for you, your company and your team is a choice you make. That choice comes in two parts: 1) Transform your team into a high-performing growth unit using time-based development sprints to ever-advance toward your customer facing-end goal positioning strategy; and 2) Leverage the 5 timeless first principles that category leaders all relied on to out-earn for shareholders and to out-build better lives for team members. **These 5 first principles are the greatest differentiators of success or lack thereof in our industry.** Bar none. The choice is now yours and we are rooting for you!

If you have questions, you will find contact information for the author in his bio on the following pages.

ABOUT THE AUTHOR

PETER LESAR IS THE CEO OF AGILITY CAPTIAL, the publicly-traded company that owns DineRock (see www.DineRock.com), the accelerator that guides restaurant businesses to upshift growth trajectories based on *how category leaders emerge as revenue & income leaders*. Peter co-founded both *Donde José,* recognized by The World's 50 Best Restaurants™ Discovery Series as one of the 50 "next generation dining destinations" around the globe, and *Lo Que Hay*, named as one the "15 best new restaurants openings" throughout the Americas (also later recognized by The World's 50 Best Restaurants™ Discovery Series). He sold both restaurants in 2019 at 6X EBITDA. Peter spent a decade on the research for this book. He can be reached at peter@agility.capital.

REFERENCES

Alan Ramadan, Dave Peterson, Christopher Lochhead and Kevin Maney. 2016. *Play Bigger: How Pirates, Dreamers, and Innovators Create and Dominate Markets.* New York: HarperCollins Publishers.

Andres, Jose, interview by Jeffrey Brown. 2020. *Celebrity chef Jose Andres on why food is a national security issue* PBS, (April 9). https://www.pbs.org/newshour/show/celebrity-chef-jose-andres-on-why-food-is-a-national-security-issue.

Barber, Dan. 2014. *The Third Plate: Field Notes on the Future of Food.* New York, New York: Penguin Audio.

Bodhipaksa. 2012. *"There are only two mistakes one can make along the road to truth: not going all the way, and not starting."* June 22. https://fakebuddhaquotes.com/there-are-only-two-mistakes-one-can-make/.

Chang, David and Meehan, Peter. 2009. *Momofuku.* New York: Absolute Press.

Churchman, C. West. 1967. "Wicked Problems." *Management Science* (University of California, Berkely) B-141 to B-146. https://pubsonline.informs.org/doi/pdf/10.1287/mnsc.14.4.B141.

Cox, Brian. Undated review. *Majordomo.* https://www.theinfatuation.com/los-angeles/reviews/majordomo.

Crosariol, Beppi. 2010. *The world's best restaurant is in ... Denmark?* October 6. https://www.theglobeandmail.com/life/travel/activities-and-interests/the-worlds-best-restaurant-is-in-denmark/article571280/.

Dave. 2006. *Thomas Keller.* October 10. https://www.powells.com/post/interviews/thomas-keller.

Drexler, Mickey, interview by David Chang. 2019. *88. The King of Retail, Mickey Drexler | The David Chang Show* The David Chang Show. December 5.

Ekstein, Nikki. 2018. *Bloomberg.* December 13. https://www.bloomberg.com/news/articles/2018-12-13/the-five-places-that-stole-my-heart-in-2018.

Epstein, David J. 2019. *Range: Why Generalists Triumph in a Specialized World.* New York: Riverhead Books.

Ferdman, Roberto A. 2015. *The Chipotle effect: Why America is obsessed with fast casual food.* Februrary 2. https://www.washingtonpost.com/news/wonk/wp/2015/02/02/the-chipotle-effect-why-america-is-obsessed-with-fast-casual-food/.

FS Blog. 2018. *Complexity Bias: Why We Prefer Complicated to Simple.* Edited by Farnham Street Media Inc. January 8. https://fs.blog/2018/01/complexity-bias/.

Goulding, Matt. 2013. *Nomanomics: How One Restaurant Is Changing Denmark's Economy.* February 14. https://world.time.com/2013/02/14/nomanomics-how-one-restaurant-is-changing-denmarks-economy/.

H.G. Parsa, John T. Self, David Njite and Tiffany King. 2005. "Why Restaurants Fail." *Cornell Hotel and Restaurant Administration Quarterly* (Cornell University) 46 (3): 304. https://journals.sagepub.com/toc/cqxa/46/3.

Hauser, Chrisine. 2020. *The Mask Slackers of 1918.* August 3. https://www.nytimes.com/2020/08/03/us/mask-protests-1918.html?auth=login-google1tap&login=google1tap.

Hayes, Adam. 2020. *Law of Diminishing Marginal Returns.* August 24. https://www.investopedia.com/terms/l/lawofdiminishingmarginalreturn.asp.

Henderson, Paul. 2018. *David Chang: "I'm not what you'd call a happy guy".* April 22. https://www.gq-magazine.co.uk/article/david-chang-interview.

Jao, Jerry. 2014. *Why Customer Retention Is King: The Evolution Of Retention Marketing.* November 19. https://www.forbes.com/sites/jerryjao/2014/11/19/why-customer-retention-is-king-the-evolution-of-retention-marketing-part-1/?sh=34219c5d186b.

Jr., Frederick F. Reicheld and W. Earl Sasser. 1990. *Zero Defections: Quality Comes to Services.* Edited by Harvard Business Publishing. September-October. https://hbr.org/1990/09/zero-defections-quality-comes-to-services.

Knowlton, Andrew. 2010. *Behind the Scenes with Chipotle Chairman and Co-CEO Steve Ells.* September 16. https://www.bonappetit.com/people/article/behind-the-scenes-with-chipotle-chairman-and-co-ceo-steve-ells.

Lonely Planet. n.d. *Donde José.* https://www.lonelyplanet.com/panama/panama-city/restaurants/donde-jose/a/poi-eat/1533228/358532.

Macrotrends. 2020. *Chipotle Mexican Grill Revenue 2006-2020 | CMG.* https://www.macrotrends.net/stocks/charts/CMG/chipotle-mexican-grill/revenue.

Meehan, Peter. 2005. *At a Noodle Bar, the Noodles Play Catch-Up.* April 13. https://www.nytimes.com/2005/04/13/dining/reviews/at-a-noodle-bar-the-noodles-play-catchup.html.

Meyer, Danny. 2006. *Setting the Table.* New York: HarperCollins Publis.

Miller, Daniel. 2020. *Before that French Laundry, there was Sally Schmitt's French Laundry.* February 21. https://www.latimes.com/food/story/2020-02-21/la-fo-french-laundry-memories.

Moskin, Julia. 2004. *Here Comes Ramen, The Slurp Heard Round the World.* November 10. https://www.nytimes.com/2004/11/10/style/dining/here-comes-ramen-the-slurp-heard-round-the-world.html?searchResultPosition=2.

New Worlder Staff. 2017. *The Best New Restaurants of 2017.* https://www.newworlder.com/article/16116/best-new-restaurants-2017.

Patronite, Rob and Raisfeld, Robin. 2015. *David Chang Opens His Spicy-Fried-Chicken-Sandwich Joint, Fuku, Today.* June 10. https://www.grubstreet.com/2015/06/david-chang-fuku-fried-chicken-opens.html.

Pomroy, Matt. 2017. *Chef Thomas Keller on Why Food Isn't The Point Of a Restaurant.* December 3. https://man.vogue.me/lifestyle/food/chef-thomas-keller-interview-bouchon/.

Price, Laura. 2016. *50 Best Stories.* November 30. https://www.theworlds50best.com/stories/news/six-of-the-most-exciting-restaurants-to-visit-in-latin-america-in-2017.html.

Restaurants, The World's 50 Best. 2016. *Discovery Series.* London: The World's 50 Best Restaurants.

Richman, Alan. 2007. *Year of the Pig.* December 12. https://www.gq.com/story/david-chang-momofuku-manhattan-chef.

Shore, Katie Rawson and Elliot. 2019. *Dining Out: A Global History of Restaurants.* London: Reaktion Books.

Skylaire, Elisabeth. n.d. *The New Nordic Food Manifesto.* https://www.norden.org/en/information/new-nordic-food-manifesto.

Sutton, Ryan. 2020. *The Legacy of David Chang's Ssäm Bar, an NYC Icon Leaving Its East Village Home.* May 19. https://ny.eater.com/2020/5/19/21263497/momofuku-ssam-bar-david-chang-closed-relocating-nyc-restaurants.

Thompson, Dereck. 2018. *Hit Makers: How to Succeed in an Age of Distraction.* New York: Penguin Books.

Watkins, D. 2020. *Chef Marcus Samuelsson: "Look out for the Black-owned restaurants ... because we need you right now".* October 31. https://www.salon.com/2020/10/31/marcus-samuelsson-the-rise-cookbook-black-chefs-list/.

Wells, Pete. 2015. *Restaurant Review: Momofuku Ko in the East Village.* October 13. https://www.nytimes.com/2015/10/14/dining/restaurant-review-momofuku-ko-east-village.html?searchResultPosition=8.

— 2019. *Why Does This Fancy Shopping Mall Smell Like Street Meat?* January 8. https://www.nytimes.com/2019/01/08/dining/momofuku-bang-bar-review.html.

Wine, Food &. 2015. *Chefs Make Change: Cat Cora for Chefs for Humanity.* March 31. https://www.foodandwine.com/news/chefs-for-humanity-cat-cora.

Yunghans, Regina. 2012. *A Brief History of Smorgasbord: It's Not Just a Buffet!* August 16. https://www.thekitchn.com/smorgasbord-not-just-a-buffet-175713.

ENDNOTES

i (Price 2016) The World's 50 Best Restaurants™ is so valuable because it shows us who is pioneering on to new ground around the world. You can look at awardees individually and break down how they are pioneers, or you can also look at them collectively to understand what the mindset of award voters is in the current era. In terms of the source cited, it should be noted that the Discovery Series for the 50 Best has been reorganized and no longer provides access to it specific recognition of Donde José in 2016. The link provided in the bibliography is related to the same year, but just speaks to those recognized in Latin America.

ii (Ekstein 2018) Media has different levels of value for restaurants. Name brand media in your market (or that targets your customers) is the most valuable, but what is even more valuable is continuing media interest in your business. Donde José was covered widely around the globe because it had a cultural truth, an a priori truth and addressed human needs in innovative ways, and that is what you need to achieve as well.

iii (New Worlder Staff 2017) *New Worlder* is a great foodie magazine for those located in or travelling to anywhere in the Americas (from Alaska to Chile). *New Worlder's* recognition of our 2nd restaurant (Lo Que Hay) as one of the most important restaurant openings of the year was great validation that our truths were applicable to different formats, meaning we could more easily find ways to scale.

iv Jose and Alberto, at the time of this book, continue to run and co-own these wonderful brands. I sold my position in 2018 to their new investors at a value greater than 6X EBITDA.

v (Jao 2014) This article was written by Jerry Jao, an expert on customer retention. Jao is the CEO of Retention Science, which offers an AI-based product that helps with engagement. Artificial intelligence is already helping the large chains, and we need to watch for AI-based systems designed for small business.

vi (Sasser 1990) I realize that the math of business in general cannot by applied to any sector specifically, including restaurants. The point is to look at the underlying case of customer and income leakage, and the financial opportunity of understanding how to turn that around not once, but always.

vii (Knowlton 2010) Many don't understand that Steve Ells is probably the greatest contributor to the rules that have shaped the fast-casual segment: Fresh ingredients, choice, fast service. Here is the interview:

https://www.bonappetit.com/people/article/behind-the-scenes-with-chipotle-chairman-and-co-ceo-steve-ells.

viii (Watkins 2020) Chef Marcus Samuelson has a rare and extraordinary background. He was born in Ethiopia and lived through the Ethiopian Civil War. He was adopted by a Swedish family and immigrated to the United States in the early 1990s. His trajectory in food in the United States has been remarkable. If you don't know him, look for his books about African American food and read his bio of accomplishments. This interview is at: https://www.salon.com/2020/10/31/marcus-samuelsson-the-rise-cookbook-black-chefs-list/.

ix (Wine 2015) Chef Cat Cora was of course the very first female Iron Chef America. She has developed and owns a series of restaurant brands and has built a successful media career (author, television host, TV personality). I believe her greatest impact is only getting started as she leads Chefs for Humanity, which works on hunger relief, nutrition education and disaster relief. Keep up to date with Chef Cora at www.catcora.com.

x (Andres 2020) Chef Jose Andres is known to almost all of us in the restaurant industry. He has been a tireless fighter on behalf of independent restaurants. Through World Central Kitchen, he has built an emergency food relief program that is a first responder to local food shortages around the world. I would have liked to cover Jose Andres more in this book, but he spends so much of his time speaking about and serving the needs of others, it has been difficult to pin down resources of what drove his restaurants. If you are feeling generous, please donate to the World Central Kitchen at https://wck.org/.

xi (Yunghans 2012) There are cited quotes are in the footnote to this paragraph, and they come from a great food magazine called *Kitchn*.

xii (Alan Ramadan 2016) If you want to understand the relevance of dominating a category, there is no better reference out there than this groundbreaking book called Play Bigger. The soft copy and hard copy have slightly different names, but seem nearly identical in content. If anyone wants to do a book group on this, let me know at the Restaurant Strong Facebook Group.

xiii (Moskin 2004) This article was written by Julia Roskin, who has been a food reporter with the New York Times since 2004. She also is a Pulitzer Prize Winner. Ironically, this 2004 article was probably assigned to her as a junior member of the team, as Chang was not yet well known. Newspaper food reporters are a fading breed, and I suggest you follow and support those few that remain. Otherwise, who will write about restaurants? You can follow Julia's social media on the bottom right of this page: https://www.nytimes.com/by/julia-moskin.

xiv (Chang 2009) Read the narrative sections of Chang's classic cookbook. Read the lines *and* between the lines and you should see how his thinking has evolved.

xv (Henderson 2018) This interview with David Chang (conducted by Paul Henderson, a food, fitness and life style Associate Editor with GQ Britain) shows how Chang thought about differentiating between fine dining and casual fine dining early on. It also shows his early thoughts on "American" cuisine. Suggest you read it here: https://www.gq-magazine.co.uk/article/david-chang-interview.

xvi (Richman 2007) This is another really valuable look at Chang's mindset as he developed. GQ produces exceptional longer-form journalism, often about our industry. Journalist Alan Richman who produced this piece is perhaps the most decorated food writer in the world (recipient of 16 James Beard Awards for journalism). He has written some of the absolute best profiles and interviews with restaurant leaders of ours, and has helped advance the careers of many of them.

xvii (Sutton 2020) Ryan Sutton's restaurant coverage (he writes for renowned *Eater*) is worth following. His social media links are here: https://www.eater.com/authors/ryan-sutton.

xviii (Wells, Restaurant Review: Momofuku Ko in the East Village 2015) Pete Wells' who wrote this article is a *New York Times* food critic and recipient of 5 James Beard Awards for Journalism. You can see his profile here: https://www.nytimes.com/by/pete-wells.

xix (Cox Undated review) Brian Cox writes some of the best restaurant reviews in Los Angeles. Here are some of his pieces on *The Infatuation*: https://www.theinfatuation.com/contributor/brant-cox.

xx (Patronite 2015) Rob Patronite and Robin Raisfeld write frequently together, covering the great New York food scene. See some of their work at https://www.grubstreet.com/author/rob-patronite/ and https://www.grubstreet.com/author/robin-raisfeld/ respectively.

xxi (Cafe n.d.) Union Square Café is a great example of leaning for years into a solution until it had been iterated so much that it had a defensive position. The awards for its popularity are the symbols of enduring focus fired up by the need of an entrepreneur to self-actualize.

xxii (Meyer 2006) The various quotes in this section come from *Setting the Table.* Again, when you pick up Meyer's book again and try to read between the lines, there is a lot of wisdom.

xxiii (Alan Ramadan 2016) While "category king" is a widely known term, it's thanks to this book that I learned how in the technology field there is such a large income spread between a category leader and its followers. I decided then to compare financial statements in the restaurant sector and noted that the trend continues there as well.

xxiv (Hassan 2020) I highly recommend this cook book as it will take you to places you haven't been before.

xxv (Hepola 2008) While this source is from an interview with Salon.com, I want to take this moment to recommend Colicchio's cook book "Think Like a Chef" because it takes you through a chef's creative process and doesn't just give you some nice recipes—a great approach.

[xxvi] (Papa John's n.d.) All of this language is taken right from Papa John's web site. If you look at product descriptions on the sites or in the materials of other leaders, you will see the same four areas addressed.

[xxvii] This quote from Chef Hall is unsourced. It is all over the Internet, but I can find no originating source. It must be in one of Chef Hall's cook books, but for the life of me I can't find it.

[xxviii] (Abraham 2013) Choi is a huge hero for me. If you don't know him, he pioneered food trucks—yes, literally. Strongly recommend you watch his series called Broken Bread, which speaks to food issues and how people in our industry are tackling some of the world's toughest challenges.